Step by Step

MEXICAN COOKING

Step by Step
MEXICAN COOKING

CHRISTINE BARRETT

PHOTOGRAPHED BY
DAVID RUSSELL

GREENWICH EDITIONS

Published 1999 by Greenwich Editions,
10 Blenheim Court, Brewery Road, London N7 9NT

© Salamander Books Ltd., 1991

ISBN 0 86288 246 X

Editor: Hilary Walden
Designer: Paul Baker
Home Economist: Gillian McCormick
Photographer: David Russell
Typeset by: Shirley Westerhoff
Colour separations by: Aero Offset (Bournemouth) Limited
Printed and bound in Spain by Bookprint, S.L.

ACKNOWLEDGEMENTS
The Publishers would like to thank the following for their help and advice:
Beales of Bournemouth
Kitchen Flair, Bournemouth, Dorset
Sabatier Knives
Braun
Le Creuset

Notes:
All spoon measurements are equal.
1 teaspoon = 5 ml spoon.
1 tablespoon = 15 ml spoon.

CONTENTS

INTRODUCTION 7

INGREDIENTS 8

EQUIPMENT 10

BASIC RECIPES 10

SOUPS 13

STARTERS 16

EGG AND CHEESE DISHES 22

FISH 26

POULTRY & MEAT 32

SAUCES 41

SALADS 44

VEGETABLES 48

DESSERTS & BAKING 53

DRINKS 61

INDEX 64

INTRODUCTION

Mexico is blessed with an abundance of varied, first-class ingredients, and a people who so enjoy food that they make full use of the ingredients to create, with infinite skill, an exciting encyclopaedia of colourful dishes. The signature of Mexican cooking are the wafts of enticing, aromatic smells that herald the rich flavours, fragrant with spices that are blended and trapped inside.

However, it is wrong to think that Mexican food is all heavily spiced and 'hot'. Some dishes have subtle flavours to allow the true taste of good quality produce to shine through, such as Vegetable Soup. When spices are added, they are used with such expertise that the flavours are mellow and harmonious. Not all dishes contain chillies and those that do can be as hot or mild as you like.

Step-by-Step Mexican Cooking shows how to make your own Tortillas, and how to transform them into an almost endless variety of dishes, such as Quesadillas, Empanadas and Burritos. And there are tantalising recipes covering the whole range of Mexican eating, some well-known, others excitingly new – free-and-easy tacos and tostados for today's favourite quick snacks, to dishes suitable for festive occasions, such as Mole Poblano, to mouthwatering vegetable and bean dishes that show vegetarian food can be fun, and, finally, a selection of delicious sweet recipes and drinks.

One of the joys of Mexican cooking is that it is easy to prepare at home; recipes are not complicated, with few exceptions ingredients are not difficult to find, and there are no fanciful arrangements, garnishes and decorations. The typical ebullient, friendly and informal Mexican personality is transferred to their food, making it an endless source of relaxed pleasure.

The style of cooking we know today as Mexican has evolved over many centuries. It is an amalgam of many influences, fused together over a period of time into a distinct, recognisable style. The foundations lie with the ancient Aztec and Mayan civilisations and the widely disparate foods available to them, such as corn (maize), avocados, fresh and dried beans, sweet potatoes, potatoes, tomatoes, chillies, pumpkins, turkeys, duck and chocolate, plus a wealth of different fish from the long coastline. From 1519, conquering Spaniards brought with them their favourite produce from the Old World - cattle, for milk and cheese as well as meat, chicken, pigs, rice, wheat, cinnamon, cloves, black pepper, oranges, peaches and apricots. The Mexicans soon adopted these 'innovations', but instead of allowing them to change their culinary traditions, they used them to enhance and extend them. In the middle of the nineteenth century, a French dimension was added, as witnessed by many of the delicious breads, cakes and puddings that are still popular.

Not surprisingly, as Mexico borders with the United States, nowadays there is a discernible American influence. The U.S. has also helped to popularise Mexican food around the world, although you are more likely to find 'TexMex' outside Mexico than in it.

BEANS

Dried beans feature prominently in the Mexican diet. Served in many ways, and incorporated into many dishes, they absorb and blend together spicy flavours, as well as adding nutritional value. Quite a number of different types of dried beans are used, but most preferred by Mexicans, such as the popular full-flavoured, smooth black beans and sweetish, soft-texture pink pinto beans, belong to the kidney beans family. Each type of bean gives its specialist character to a dish, however if a specified type is not available, red kidney beans could be substituted, as a variation.

CHEESE

A crumbly, quite salty white cheese, queso fresco is the most frequently used in Mexico. Good Wensleydale, Cheshire, Lancashire or Greek feta are the best substitutes. Queso de Chihuahua is also popular. A mixture of cheddar and mozzarella make a good alternative.

CHILLIES

Chillies are a hall-mark of Mexican cooking, being used both raw and cooked to give a distinctive flavour as well as hotness.

There are many different varieties of chilli, but only a relatively few are available outside Mexico, and in Britain the choice is quite limited. The most commonly found and used varieties are:-

Dried – are the most commonly used variety in Mexico. They are mild, with a fragrance reminiscent of prunes and raisins, wrinkled and deep reddish brown, about 13 cm (5 in) long and 7.5 cm (3 in) wide.

Mulato – are similar in appearance to ancho chillies, but sweeter.

Pasilla – are long, thin brownish-black with a fruity piquant flavour.

Jalepeno - are dark rich green and hot, although not as hot as serranos. They are about 6.5 cm (2¹/₂ in) long and 2 cm (³/₄ in) wide. If unable to buy fresh jalepenos, look for canned ones, but be sure to rinse well before using.

Serrano – are small, light green, shiny and smooth, and very hot. They are also available in cans.

Chillies are not always labelled with their variety, so as a general guide, dried chillies have a more earthy, fruity flavour than fresh ones, smaller varieties are invariably hotter than large ones, but red chillies are not always hotter than green.

The seeds and white veins are not only hotter than the flesh, but have less flavour, and are generally removed from the chilli before using.

Chillies contain an oil that can make the eyes and even the skin sting, so always avoid touching the eyes after touching chillies.

To be really safe, wear rubber gloves when preparing chillies.

In preparing the recipes for this book, unless a variety has been specified, fairly large, quite mild green chillies were used.

Other varieties can be substituted according to taste, or what is available. For more flavour and heat, use a hotter variety, or increase the level.

Further ways to adjust the 'heat' of cooked dishes are:-

1. For flavour without too much heat use the chilli whole and remove on completion of cooking.

2. For medium-heat, add several whole chillies and one chilli halved lengthways and seeds discarded. Discard chillies before serving dish.

3. For hot dishes, add chopped or sliced chillies, with or without seeds, remembering that the more seed you add, the hotter the dish.

In Mexico a bowl of pickled jalepeno chillies or a hot relish such as hot chilli sauce, are put on the table so people can add extra 'hotness' if desired.

INGREDIENTS

CHILLI POWDER

Chilli powder adds an extra flavour dimension to the hotness because in addition to ground dried chillies, it may contain ground cumin and salt and perhaps other seasonings. Chilli powder should be added gradually.

HOT PEPPER SAUCE

Hot pepper sauce which is made from a blend of chillies and seasonings, also adds a particular flavour, as well as hotness. There are several brands and each will have its own particular intensity and flavour.

CHAYOTE

Chayote is a type of squash also known as christophene, resembling a ridged-pear with a pale green, fairly thick skin, and crisp white, delicately flavoured flesh. Chayotes weigh between 6 to 12 ounces. Although a fruit, they are eaten as a vegetable, sometimes raw in salads, but more often baked, stuffed, added to casseroles or boiled (they can be peeled before or after cooking). The seed of young chayote is edible.

COOKING FAT

Good pork lard is the preferred choice for cooking in Mexico, but because it is not always available, and not to everybody's taste, vegetable oils and butter are usually used in this book. However, good quality lard can be substituted for a true Mexican flavour when frying.

CORN HUSKS

Corn husks are the dried outer leaves of ears of corn and are used to make tamales. They can be bought ready dried but if unavailable a good substitute is to put squares of waxed paper inside squares of foil.

CREAM

Mexican cream is similar to French crème fraîche. which is available in some supermarkets and gourmet stores, or can be made at home by stirring a tablespoonful of natural yogurt into whipping cream and leaving, covered, overnight. Alternatively, use thick sour cream.

MASA HARINA

Masa harina is a type of flour that is made from corn that has been steeped and boiled in lime, dried and very finely ground. It is paler than normal cornmeal and produces heavy doughs. It is used for Corn Tortillas and Tamales. Masa harina is available in most large supermarkets.

TOMATILLOS

Tomatillos belong to the same family as Cape gooseberries, and look like green cherry tomatoes covered in a papery outer casing. They are sometimes referred to as green tomatoes. Their characteristic texture and citrus tang lend body and freshness to dishes. They are usually cooked to develop their lemon-herb flavour and soften their flesh, but occasionally are eaten raw when their sharpness is beneficial, such as in Salsa Verde.

Search for canned tomatillos in speciality food shops if fresh are unavailable. Unripe green ordinary tomatoes are not a good substitute.

TOMATOES

Mexican tomatoes are large and irregularly shaped, similar to beef steak or Mediterranean tomatoes. For the most authentic Mexican flavour, use sun-ripened tomatoes rather than greenhouse-grown ones. If unavailable canned, peeled plum tomatoes can be substituted when making sauces, the most popular way of using tomatoes in Mexico.

TORTILLAS

Tortillas are eaten with meals in the same way as bread, as well as being an integral part of many other dishes.

Corn Tortillas are the traditional version, but in the north of Mexico, near the American border, Wheat Tortillas are now made. They are more difficult to make and quickly become brittle if overcooked, and, so, difficult to fold. They are also more filling.

Tortillas that have been prepared in advance, and are therefore cold, are heated before using, usually in hot oil or on a hot griddle or in a frying pan, to make them pliable. A microwave oven can also be used.

There are no hard and fast rules governing the choice of fillings and toppings. They can be varied, mixed and matched to taste. For example, Refried Beans, Picadillo or shredded chicken, turkey or ham, bound with cream cheese, or topped with Salsa Fresca or Salsa Verde or Guacamole. Or perhaps sliced chorizo (spicy Spanish sausage) or diced cheese mixed with cream cheese.

Burritos – are soft, filled and rolled tortillas.

Enchiladas – are filled, rolled tortillas, covered with a sauce and baked.

Nachos – are fried tortilla chips topped with cheese and chillies, then grilled until the cheese melts.

Quesadillas – are really like tortilla sandwiches which are sold by street vendors and eaten in the open air. They are often filled with green chillies and cheese and then heated.

Tacos – are soft or crisp tortillas that are filled with a sauce and meat mixture, then folded or rolled. These are eaten from your hand.

Tortilla Chips – or totopos are tortillas cut in about eight wedges, then fried until crisp. Tortilla chips are frequently served with dips, such as Guacamole and Bean Dip.

Tostadas – are fried flat tortillas that are topped with beans or meat, lettuce and cheese.

SPECIAL EQUIPMENT

There are only two pieces of special equipment required for Mexican cooking:-

Blender or food processor – invaluable for eliminating the great deal of pounding in a pestle and mortar that takes place in a traditional Mexican kitchen.

Tortilla press – the best way to ensure thin, home-made corn tortillas, which is not easy by hand. They are available from specialist kitchenware shops and departments in large stores.

To use a tortilla press, line the bottom plate of the press with a square of greaseproof paper or plastic. Flatten to a thick circle a piece of dough about the size of a small egg, place on the paper or wrap, and cover with another piece of greaseproof paper or plastic wrap. Close the press, pressing the handle down firmly. Open the press, remove the top sheet of paper or plastic, then, using the bottom sheet, lift off the tortilla and invert onto a hot griddle or into a frying pan.

CORN TORTILLAS

315 g (10 oz/2 ½ cups) masa harina
  (maize flour)
1 teaspoon salt
about 280 ml (9 fl oz/1 ¼ cups) warm water

In a large bowl, mix together masa harina and salt. Gradually stir in sufficient warm water to make a soft but not sticky dough. Divide dough into 12 pieces. To shape by hand, form one piece of dough into a ball, flatten slightly then put on a piece of waxed paper. Put a second piece of waxed paper over the top and roll out to circle of desired size. Stack between the sheets of waxed paper.

To shape, use a tortilla press. Heat a griddle or heavy frying pan over a medium heat until a few drops of cold water will sizzle when sprinkled on it. Carefully peel off the bottom sheet of waxed paper and place tortilla gently on griddle or in pan. Cook for 1 minute, until edges begin to curl, then remove top piece of waxed paper and, using a spatula, turn over tortilla. Cook for 1 minute. The first side to be cooked is the top and should be slightly puffy and speckled brown. Stack tortillas on a wire rack covered with a tea-towel.

Cover with another tea-towel. The tortillas are now ready to eat, fry, refrigerate or freeze.

Makes twelve 15 cm (6 in) tortillas.

Note: Corn tortillas can be kept in a sealed plastic bag in the refrigerator for up to 10 days, or frozen interleaved with waxed paper, in a sealed plastic bag for 3 months.

WHEAT TORTILLAS

315 g (10 oz/2²/3 cups) wholemeal flour
1 teaspoon salt
45 g (1¹/2 oz) lard, diced
315 ml (10 fl oz/1¹/4 cups) hot water

Put flour and salt in a large mixing bowl. Rub the fat in until mixture resembles breadcrumbs. Stir in hot water to form a soft, pliable dough. On a floured board, knead dough until smooth, then cover with a warm, damp tea-towel.

Divide dough into 12 pieces. Shape one piece into a ball, then flatten. Place on a floured board, using a floured rolling pin, and keeping a circular shape, roll out very thinly so the board can be seen through the dough. Trim edges if necessary. Stack on a floured plate, making sure there is enough flour on each one to prevent sticking. Heat a griddle or heavy frying pan until a few drops of water will sizzle when sprinkled on, then reduce heat slightly. Carefully put a tortilla on the griddle or into pan.

Leave for 30 seconds, until beginning to bubble, turn over and cook for 10 seconds more. It will look pale and undercooked, but if cooked for longer, it will become dry and brittle. Stack tortillas on a wire rack covered with a tea towel, and cover with another tea towel.

Note: To store, leave to cool, still covered, then place a square of waxed paper between each one to prevent sticking, store in a sealed plastic bag, in the refrigerator for 2-3 days.

Makes twelve 15 cm (6 in) tortillas.

BASIC BEANS

500 g (1 lb) pinto beans, soaked overnight
2 tablespoons beef dripping
1 small onion, chopped
salt

Drain the beans and rinse. Put in a large saucepan, cover well with cold water, bring to the boil. Boil for 10 minutes, partly cover the pan with the lid and cook at a rolling boil for up to 3 hours or until the beans are very soft. Top up with boiling water if necessary.

Heat dripping and fry onion until golden. Add to beans, season with salt and simmer for 15 minutes or until the bean liquid thickens. Use immediately or cool and store in a covered container in the refrigerator for 2 days.

Serves 8.

REFRIED BEANS

2 tablespoons oil
½ quantity Basic Beans
60 g (2 oz) grated *queso fresco*, Lancashire,
Cheshire or Wensleydale cheese to serve

Heat the oil in a frying pan over a medium heat.
Add the beans and mash together with a fork
to make a thick paste. If mixture sticks, add
another tablespoon of oil.

Serve sprinkled with grated cheese.

Serves 4.

Variations: Re-fried beans can be used without the cheese. They may also be served as a
side dish to a main course.

COOKED TOMATO SAUCE

1 tablespoon olive oil
1 small onion, finely chopped
1 clove garlic, finely chopped
500 g (1 lb) tomatoes, blanched, skinned, chopped
1 fresh green chilli
1 tablespoon tomato purée (paste)
1 teaspoon finely chopped fresh coriander
salt and pepper

Heat oil in a frying pan and fry onion and garlic for 5 minutes until soft but not brown.
Add tomatoes, chilli, tomato purée (paste)
and coriander; season with salt and pepper.

Simmer for 20 minutes or until thick.
Remove the chilli. For a 'hot' sauce chop the
chilli and return to the sauce.

Makes 500 ml (16 fl oz / 2 cups)

PICADILLO

250 g (8 oz) minced beef
250 g (8 oz) minced pork
2 tablespoons red wine vinegar
salt and pepper
1 tablespoon oil
1 small onion, finely chopped
1 clove garlic, finely chopped
1 fresh green chilli, finely chopped
500 g (1 lb) tomatoes, skinned, chopped
60 g (2 oz/1/3 cup) seedless raisins
60 g (2 oz/1/2 cup) slivered almonds
1/2 teaspoon ground cloves
1 teaspoon ground cinnamon
2 tablespoons tomato purée (paste)

Mix meats together with vinegar, salt and pepper. Heat the oil in a frying pan, add the onion, garlic and chilli and fry for 3 minutes, stirring frequently. Add the meat mixture and stir over a high heat until beginning to brown. Drain off the fat.

Stir in the tomatoes, raisins, almonds, ground cloves, cinnamon and tomato purée (paste). Simmer for 15 minutes, uncovered, or until the mixture is thick and well blended. Use hot as a filling for tortillas, enchiladas, chimichangas, burritos or taco shells, or use cold as a filling for empanadas.

Serves 4-6.

VERMICELLI SOUP

2 tablespoons oil
60 g (2 oz) vermicelli
1 medium onion, chopped
1 clove garlic, finely chopped
500 g (1 lb) tomatoes, peeled, seeded and chopped
2 litres (64 fl oz/8 cups) beef stock
salt and pepper
60 ml (2 fl oz/1/4 cup) dry sherry
1 tablespoon finely chopped fresh coriander to garnish
grated Parmesan cheese to serve

Heat oil in a frying pan over medium low heat. Add vermicelli and fry for 2-3 minutes until golden. Drain the vermicelli and set aside; reserve oil. Place onion, garlic, salt and tomatoes in a blender or food processor and process until smooth. Heat reserved oil in the frying pan over medium heat, then pour in tomato mixture. Cook for 5 minutes, stirring constantly.

Put vermicelli, tomato mixture and stock into a large saucepan. Season with salt and pepper. Cover and bring slowly to the boil, then simmer for 10 minutes until vermicelli is tender. Stir in sherry. Pour into a warmed tureen. Garnish with chopped coriander. Serve with grated Parmesan cheese.

Serves 6-8.

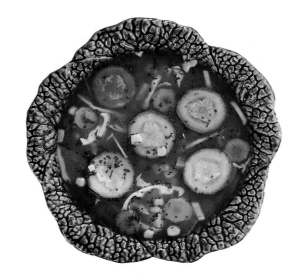

— CHICKEN TORTILLA SOUP —

940 ml (30 fl oz/3 ³/4 cups) chicken stock
1 pasilla chilli
2 tablespoons oil
4 Corn Tortillas, cut into 1 cm (¹/2in) strips
   (¹/2 in) strips
¹/2 onion, finely chopped
185 g (6 oz) cooked chicken, shredded
2 tablespoons fresh lime juice
salt and pepper

Boil 155 ml (5 fl oz/¹/3 cup) of chicken stock. Place chilli in a small bowl, pour boiling stock over and leave for 30 minutes. Drain; reserve the stock. Discard the stem and seeds of the chilli; chop the flesh finely. Reserve.

Heat the oil in a heavy frying pan and fry the tortilla strips until golden. Drain on absorbent kitchen paper. Add the onion to the oil left in the pan; or add a little more if necessary. Gently fry the onion for about 4 minutes until soft but not brown. Add all the stock and simmer for 10 minutes, skimming off any foam that comes to the surface. Add the chicken and lime juice and season with salt and pepper; simmer for 5 minutes.

Place the tortilla strips in a warmed soup tureen or individual bowls, and pour over the hot soup. Garnish with the reserved chopped chilli.

Serves 6 .

— VEGETABLE SOUP —

1 litre (32 fl oz/4 cups) chicken stock
500 ml (16 fl oz/2 cups) water
500 g (1 lb) tomatoes, peeled and chopped
1 large onion, finely chopped
1 clove garlic, crushed with 1 teaspoon salt
8 whole black peppercorns
4 whole cloves
250 g (8 oz) potato, cubed
125 g (4 oz) courgettes (zucchini), sliced
315 g (10 oz) white cabbage, coarsely sliced
125 g (4 oz) carrot, sliced
125 g (4 oz) celery, thinly sliced
125 g (4 oz) sweetcorn kernels
chopped coriander to garnish

Place the chicken stock, water, tomatoes, onion and garlic in a large saucepan. Tie the peppercorns and cloves in a piece of muslin and add to the pan. Bring to the boil, cover, then simmer for 40 minutes. Add the potato, courgettes (zucchini), cabbage, carrots, celery and sweetcorn. Cover and simmer for about 10 minutes or until all the vegetables are tender. Discard the muslin bag.

Pour the soup into a warmed tureen and garnish with chopped coriander.

Serves 6-8 .

AVOCADO SOUP

2 large avocado pears
315 ml (10 fl oz/1 ¼ cups) double (thick) cream
1 litre (32 fl oz/4 cups) chicken stock
3 tablespoons dry sherry
salt
2 tablespoons chopped coriander, to garnish

Cut the avocados in half lengthways, remove the stones and scoop the flesh into blender or food processor. Add half of the cream and process until smooth. Add half of the remaining cream and process again until just combined. Place the chicken stock in a medium sized saucepan and bring slowly to the boil.

Remove from the heat and gradually whisk in the avocado purée. Add the sherry. Heat gently, but do not boil. Season with salt. Remove from the heat. Pour into a warmed soup tureen. Serve hot or cold with the remaining cream swirled over the top and chopped coriander sprinkled over.

Serves 4-6.

SOPA FRIJOLES

175 g (6 oz) dried red kidney beans, soaked
    overnight
1.25 litres (40 fl oz/5 cups) water
1 medium onion, chopped
1 clove garlic, crushed
1 ½ teaspoons chilli powder
salt
60 g (2 oz) Mozzarella cheese, grated
125 g (4 oz) croûtons

Drain the beans and rinse well under cold running water. In a large saucepan, bring the water to the boil. Add the beans. Bring slowly to the boil, then simmer for 2 hours, or until the beans are tender.

Add the onion, garlic and chilli powder, and simmer for a further 30-40 minutes. Place in a blender or food processor and process until smooth; this may have to be done in batches. Add more water if necessary. Return the soup to the saucepan and re-heat.

Season with salt. Serve in a warmed soup tureen with cheese sprinkled over and garnished with croûtons.

Serves 4.

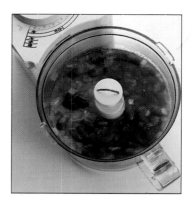

CORN SOUP

30 g (1 oz/2 tablespoons) butter
1 small onion, finely chopped
1 clove garlic crushed in 5 ml/1 teaspoon salt
3 small tomatoes, blanched, skinned and chopped
2 litres (40 fl oz/5 cups) chicken stock
1 bay leaf
250 g (8 oz) sweetcorn kernels
salt and pepper
155 ml (5 fl oz/²/₃ cup) single (light) cream
2 tablespoons chopped fresh coriander

In a large saucepan melt the butter. Add the onion and garlic and cook gently for about 5 minutes until the onion is soft but not brown. Add the tomatoes. Simmer gently for 10 minutes, breaking down the tomatoes with a spoon. Add the stock, bay leaf and sweetcorn kernels. Season to taste. Bring to the boil, then reduce the heat and simmer for 30 minutes. Discard the bay leaf. Pour the soup in a blender or food processor and process well until smooth; this may have to be done in batches.

Return the soup to the saucepan. Stir in the cream and heat gently to just below boiling point; do not allow the soup to boil. Serve in a warmed tureen with chopped coriander sprinkled over.

Serves 6.

— PRAWNS WITH CHILLI CHEESE —

½ quantity Cooked Tomato Sauce
155 ml (5 fl oz/²/₃ cup) thick sour cream
few drops of Tabasco sauce
60 g (2 oz) Cheddar cheese, grated
1 fresh green chilli, finely chopped
salt
24 large cooked prawns in their shells
lemon wedges to garnish

In a bowl, combine all the ingredients except the prawns and lemon wedges. Adjust seasonings to taste.

Serve the dip in individual ramekin dishes on a plate with the prawns round the outside, tails facing inwards. Garnish with wedges of lemon.

Serves 6.

Note: The dip may also be served with tortilla chips.

GUACAMOLE

½ small onion, finely chopped
4 tomatoes, skinned, seeded and finely chopped
1 fresh green chilli, seeded and finely chopped
½ small green pepper (capsicum), seeded and
    finely chopped
1 tablespoon chopped coriander
2 large ripe avocado pears
salt and pepper
2 teaspoons lemon juice
1 tablespoon olive oil
tortilla chips or crudités to serve

In a bowl, mix together onion, tomato, chilli, green pepper (capsicum) and coriander. Cut the avocados in half lengthways, remove the stone, and scoop out the flesh.

Mash roughly with tomato mixture. Season with salt and pepper, and stir in the lemon juice. Transfer to a serving bowl and sprinkle with olive oil. Serve immediately with tortilla chips or crudité.

Serves 6.

MARINATED MUSHROOMS

2 tablespoons olive oil
1 clove garlic
250 g (8 oz) mushrooms, thickly sliced
1 medium onion, thinly sliced
1 carrot, finely grated
1 stick celery, thinly sliced
1 green pepper (capsicum), seeded and thinly
    sliced
1 fresh green chilli, seeded, finely chopped
1½ tablespoons lemon juice
1 tablespoon chopped fresh coriander
salt and pepper

Heat the oil in a heavy frying pan, and gently fry the garlic until brown. Discard the garlic. To the pan, add mushrooms, onion, carrot, celery, pepper (capsicum) and chilli. Fry gently for 5 minutes. Add lime or lemon juice and coriander and season with salt and pepper.

Cover and simmer for 5 minutes. Cool completely, then transfer to a serving bowl.

Serves 4.

BEANDIP

60 g (2 oz/4 tablespoons) butter
1 small onion, chopped
1 garlic clove, chopped
1 teaspoon ground cinnamon
1 teaspoon chilli powder
½ teaspoon ground cumin
½ quantity Basic Beans
60 g (2 oz) mature Cheddar cheese, grated.
salt
Tabasco sauce, if desired
tortilla chips, to serve

In a saucepan, melt butter, add onion, garlic, chilli powder and cumin. Fry gently for 10 minutes until onion has softened. Add Basic Beans and cheese and stir until melted.

Turn mixture into a blender or food processor and process until smooth; this may have to be done in batches. Taste, add salt if necessary, add Tabasco sauce if desired. If the mixture is too thick, add water 1 tablespoon at a time. Turn into a serving dish. Serve with tortilla chips.

Serves 6-8.

CEVICHE

500 g (1 lb) firm white fish fillets such as haddock, cod or bass
90 ml (3 fl oz/⅓ cup) fresh lime juice
155 ml (5 fl oz/⅔ cup) olive oil
2 spring onions, finely chopped
1 clove garlic, finely chopped
2 tablespoons finely chopped fresh coriander
few drops of Tabasco sauce
sea salt

Rinse fish, dry and cut into thin strips across the grain. Place in a non-metallic bowl. Pour over lime juice, cover and marinate for at least 15 minutes, but preferably overnight in a cool place, when the fish will become opaque. In a serving bowl combine olive oil, spring onion, garlic, half the coriander and Tabasco sauce. Season with salt.

Drain fish and add to serving bowl. Toss gently, making sure fish is well coated. Sprinkle with remaining coriander.

Serves 6.

Variation: Use 375 g (12 oz) shelled scallops instead of white fish; slice each horizontally into two or three even slices.

MEATBALL KEBABS

4 small courgettes (zucchini)
125 g (4 oz) button mushrooms
125 g (4 oz) cherry tomatoes
250 g (8 oz) minced lamb or beef
1 small onion, finely chopped
1 tablespoon finely chopped coriander
¼ teaspoon ground cumin
large pinch cayenne pepper
1 egg, beaten
salt and pepper
oil for brushing on vegetables

Cut the courgettes (zucchini) into 2.5 cm (1 in) chunks, then steam for 5 minutes. Drain. Using a teaspoon scoop out 1 cm (½ in) of flesh from one end. Remove mushroom stalks, finely chop, and reserve. Slice tops off tomatoes; using a teaspoon carefully scoop out seeds. In a medium bowl, combine meat, onion, coriander, cumin, cayenne pepper, egg, and mushroom stalks. Season with salt and pepper.

Pre-heat grill to the hottest setting.

Fill courgettes (zucchini), tomatoes and mushroom caps with the meat mixture, and thread alternately on to skewers so they are touching closely. Brush with olive oil and grill for 10 minutes each side, making sure they do not burn – reduce heat if necessary.

Serves 6

Note: Any left-over mixture can be fried and served with tortilla chips.

STUFFED EGGS

1 medium avocado pear
6 hard-boiled eggs, halved lengthways
1 small onion, very finely chopped
1 small green pepper (capsicum), seeded and very finely chopped
125 g (4 oz) cooked prawns, shelled, deveined and chopped
1 teaspoon lemon juice
1 teaspoon white wine vinegar
salt and pepper
large pinch cayenne pepper
shredded lettuce and sliced tomato to serve
1 tablespoon finely chopped coriander, to garnish

Cut the avocado in half lengthways, remove the stone and scoop the flesh into a food processor or blender. Using a teaspoon, scoop out the egg yolks into the food processor or blender; blend until smooth.

Transfer to a medium bowl. Stir in the onion, green pepper (capsicum), prawns, lemon juice, vinegar, salt, pepper and cayenne pepper. Using a teaspoon, place generous amounts of the mixture into the egg whites. Arrange on a bed of shredded lettuce and tomato slices. Sprinkle with coriander.

Serves 6

STUFFED ROAST BEEF ROLLS

6 oz (185 g) courgettes (zuchini), peeled and
    sliced
1 medium avocado pear
60 g (2 oz) onion, very finely chopped
½ teaspoon chilli powder
2 tablespoons olive oil
2 tablespoons white wine vinegar
salt
16 thin slices cold roast beef
lettuce leaves
3 hard-boiled eggs, halved lengthways
radishes to garnish

Steam the courgette (zuchini) slices over
boiling, salted water for about 3 minutes
until tender; cool completely. Cut avocado
in half lengthways, discard stone and scoop
flesh into a blender or food processor.
Add courgettes (zuchini) and process until
smooth. Transfer to a medium bowl. Stir in
onion, chilli powder, oil and vinegar. Mix
well and season with salt. Place a tablespoon
of the mixture on each slice of beef, roll up
and secure with a cocktail stick; reserve any
remaining avocado mixture.

Place lettuce leaves on a flat serving plate.
Arrange the beef rolls in a circle, like the
spokes of a wheel. Scoop out and sieve egg
yolks. Place in the centre of the serving
dish. Cut egg whites into thin strips and
place on the roast beef rolls. Garnish with
radishes. Serve any reserved avocado mixture separately.

Serves 8 .

NACHOS

sunflower oil for frying
6 Corn Tortillas

Topping:
90 g (3 oz) Cheddar cheese, grated
1 medium onion, finely chopped
1 fresh green pepper (capsicum), seeded and finely
    chopped
1 green chilli, finely chopped
1 pickled jalapeño chilli, finely chopped,
    if desired
1 teaspoon chilli powder
155 ml (5 fl oz/²/₃ cup) thick sour cream

Pour oil into a large heavy frying pan to a
depth of 2.5 cm (1 in). Heat the oil, and
when it is hot, lower a tortilla into the oil
using tongs. When tortilla turns golden
brown and is crisp, remove quickly and
drain on absorbent kitchen paper. Keep
warm. Repeat with remaining tortillas. Pre-
heat the grill to its hottest setting.

Break each tortilla into eight pieces and lay
in a single layer on the base of a grill pan.
Put a layer of grated cheese on each piece
of tortilla, then a layer of onion, then
green pepper (capsicum), then the chilli and
jalapeño chilli, if used. Sprinkle with chilli
powder and spoon a little sour cream over
the top. Put under the grill for 4-5 minutes
until the sour cream is bubbling and the
cheese has melted, lower the heat if necessary.

Serves 6.

SAVOURY TAMALES

30 dried corn husks, soaked overnight in cold water (see Note)
375 g (12 oz) cooked chicken, shredded

Filling:
500 g (1 lb) green tomatillos, blanched and skinned
½ onion, chopped
12 sprigs fresh coriander
salt and pepper
1 tablespoon olive oil

Dough:
375 g (12 oz) masa harina (maize flour)
salt
2 teaspoons baking powder
375 ml (12 fl oz/1 ½ cups) warm water
125 g (4 oz) lard, softened
315 ml (10 fl oz/1 ¼ cups) warm meat stock

To make filling, put the tomatillos into a saucepan, just cover with water and bring to the boil. Simmer for 5 minutes. Drain; reserve liquid.

In a blender or food processor, mix the tomatillos, coriander, salt, pepper and enough of the reserved liquid to make a fairly thick paste. Heat the oil in a heavy frying pan and fry the onion for 2-3 minutes. Stir in the tomatillo paste and simmer for about 20 minutes, adding more liquid if necessary to maintain a fairly thick paste. Set aside.

To make a dough, in a bowl mix together the masa harina (maize flour), salt, water and lard. Slowly stir in the stock. Add the baking powder and beat with a wooden spoon until bubbles appear and a teaspoonful dropped in a glass of cold water floats and sticks together. Drain and pat dry the corn husks. Place 2 husks overlapping in the palm of one hand and spoon on 1 tablespoon of sauce, 1 tablespoon dough, a little cooked chicken, and another spoonful of sauce.

Wrap the husks carefully to enclose the filling, then fold tail towards the top leaving it loose to allow room for expansion. Place tamales in the top half of a steamer and cover with greaseproof paper. Cover tightly and steam for 1 ½ hours until dough is light and fluffy. Re-heat any remaining sauce and serve separately.

Serves 6.

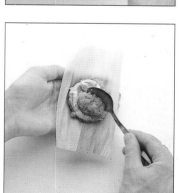

Variations: Substitute Cooked Tomato Sauce for the tomatillo sauce. Use cooked pork, beef, fish or turkey instead of chicken.

Note: If dried corn husks are not available, use thirty 20 cm (8 in) squares of foil covered with squares of waxed paper. Place prepared sauce, dough, chicken, then more sauce in centre. Fold foil over loosely, sealing edges securely to make them water tight.

CORN SOUFFLÉ

60 g (2 oz/4 tablespoons) butter
½ medium onion, finely chopped
250 g (8 oz) sweetcorn kernels
3 eggs, separated
2 fresh green chillies, seeded and chopped
salt

Pre-heat the oven to 190°C (375°F/ Gas 5). Grease a 20 cm (8 in) soufflé dish, and sprinkle the inside lightly with flour.

In a medium saucepan, melt butter. Add onion and cook for about 4 minutes until soft but not brown. Transfer to a blender or food processor. Add sweetcorn and egg yolks. Process until as smooth as possible. Transfer to a large bowl. Stir in the chillies and salt.

In a bowl, whisk the egg whites until stiff. Gently fold into corn mixture until just evenly mixed. Transfer mixture to the soufflé dish. Bake for 10 minutes; reduce temperature to 180°C (350°F/Gas 4) and bake for a further 20-30 minutes until lightly brown, and just set in the centre. Serve immediately.

Serves 4.

EGGS VALLEJO-STYLE

30 g (1 oz/2 tablespoons) butter
1 small onion, thinly sliced
1 fresh green chilli, seeded, cut in strips
500 g (1 lb) tomatoes, skinned, seeded and chopped
2 tablespoons tomato purée (paste)
salt and pepper
6 eggs
90 g (3 oz) Cheddar cheese, grated

Melt butter in a large, heavy frying pan. Add onion and cook over medium heat until soft but not brown. Stir in chilli, tomatoes and tomato purée (paste). Simmer for 10 minutes.

Season with salt and pepper. Make four indentations in mixture. Break the eggs one at a time onto a saucer, then carefully slide into indentations, cover and simmer for about 4 minutes until the egg whites are almost set.

Top each egg with cheese, cover and cook for 1 minute until cheese has melted. Serve immediately.

Serves 6.

RANCH-STYLE EGGS

EGGS WITH POTATOES & HAM

1 quantity Cooked Tomato Sauce
½ quantity Re-fried Beans
sunflower oil for frying
8 Corn or Wheat Tortillas
8 eggs
2 thin slices cooked ham, diced
125 g (4 oz) cooked fresh, or thawed frozen peas
1 banana to garnish

In separate saucepans, gently heat Tomato Sauce, and Re-fried Beans. Keep hot.

Pour oil into a heavy frying pan to a depth of 5 mm (¼ in) and heat to 185°C (360°F). Fry each tortilla for 1-1½ minutes until crisp and brown. Drain on absorbent kitchen paper. Keep tortilla warm. Fry the eggs in same oil. Divide half of the Tomato Sauce between four warmed plates.

Place a spoonful of Re-fried Beans on the sauce, then top with a tortilla. Place 2 eggs side by side on the tortilla and cover with a second tortilla. Spoon over the remaining Tomato Sauce.

Sprinkle with ham and peas. Peel and slice the banana then scatter over to garnish.

Serves 4.

2 large or 4 medium baking potatoes, peeled
2 tablespoons oil
1 small onion, finely chopped
125 g (4 oz) cooked lean ham
4 eggs
1 avocado pear and coriander sprigs to garnish

Cut potatoes into 5 mm (¼ in) slices, then into 5 mm (¼ in) dice. Rinse with cold water. Drain well and dry on absorbent kitchen paper.

Heat oil in a heavy frying pan. Add potato and onion, cover and cook over a medium heat, shaking pan frequently until tender, about 15 minutes. Add the ham, mix well and heat for 5 minutes.

With the back of a large spoon, make four indentations in the mixture. Break eggs one at a time onto a saucer then carefully slide into each indentation. Cover, and cook until eggs are set, about 5 minutes. Peel, stone and slice the avocado. Serve the eggs and potatoes garnished with avocado slices and coriander.

Serves 4.

— EGG-FILLED ENCHILADAS —

1 quantity Cooked Tomato Sauce
75 ml (2 ¹/₂ fl oz/¹/₃ cup) sunflower oil
8 Wheat Tortillas
4 eggs
155 ml (5 fl oz/²/₃ cup) thick sour cream
salt and pepper
2 tablespoons chopped fresh coriander to garnish

Pre-heat oven 190°C (375°F/Gas 5). Grease a shallow ovenproof dish.

In a saucepan over low heat, warm cooked Tomato Sauce, stirring occasionally. Meanwhile, heat oil in a heavy frying pan. Using tongs, carefully place one tortilla at a time in hot oil, hold in the oil for 3-5 seconds until soft, then turn over and repeat on the second side. Drain on absorbent kitchen paper and keep warm.

Mash eggs and sour cream in a bowl, season with salt and pepper. Spoon onto tortillas and roll up. Place seam-side down in ovenproof dish. Pour over Tomato Sauce. Cover with foil and bake for 15-20 minutes to heat through. Garnish with coriander and serve immediately.

Serves 4.

CHIMICHANGAS

12 Wheat Tortillas
oil for deep frying
Guacamole
155 ml (5 fl oz/²/₃ cup) thick sour cream
250 g (8 oz) Cheddar cheese, grated
1 tablespoon oil
1 small onion, finely chopped
1 clove garlic, finely chopped
1 green chilli, seeded and finely chopped
1 jalapeño chilli, finely chopped
½ green pepper (capsicum), cored, seeded, finely chopped
2 medium potatoes, diced and boiled

To prepare the filling, heat the oil in a small frying pan. Add the onion, garlic, chillies and pepper (capsicum). Fry gently over medium heat for about 4 minutes until soft but not brown. Add potato and mix well. Set to one side. Heat a heavy frying pan until drops of water will sizzle when sprinkled on. Place a tortilla in the pan to warm for 30 seconds. Turn. Place a spoonful of onion mixture in centre, top with a spoonful of sour cream then grated cheese. Fold to a parcel and secure with a cocktail stick. Repeat with the tortillas. Refrigerate for 30 minutes.

Heat the oil in the deep fat frying pan. Fry the chimichangas a few at a time, for about 5 minutes until golden brown. Drain on absorbent kitchen paper; keep warm. Alternatively, shallow fry for 3 minutes on each side and drain.

Discard cocktail sticks and serve hot with Guacamole.

Serves 6.

— CHEESE-FILLED ENCHILADAS —

3 tablespoons sunflower oil
12 Wheat or Corn Tortillas
1 quantity Cooked Tomato Sauce
1 teaspoon hot chilli powder
1 oz (30 g) Parmesan cheese, grated
1 tablespoon chopped fresh coriander

Filling:
750 g (1 ½ lbs) cottage, quark, or low fat curd
    cheese or any combination of these
375 g (12 oz) *queso fresco*, Lancashire, Cheshire
    or Wensleydale cheese, grated
1 ½ teaspoons mustard powder
2 cloves garlic, finely chopped
pepper

Pre-heat the oven to 190°C (375°F/Gas 5). Grease a large, shallow ovenproof dish.

To make the filling, mix all ingredients in a bowl; set aside. Heat oil in a heavy frying pan. Using tongs, carefully place one tortilla at a time in the hot oil. Hold for 3-5 seconds until softened, Quickly turn over the tortilla and repeat on the second side. Drain on absorbent kitchen paper and then wrap in a napkin to keep warm. Cook each tortilla in the same way, wrapping in the napkin to keep warm.

Divide the filling between the warm tortillas, roll up and pack together, seam-side down, in the dish. Stir chilli powder into Cooked Tomato Sauce, pour over enchiladas, and sprinkle with cheese. Cover with foil and bake for 45 minutes. Remove the foil and bake for a further 15 minutes to brown. Remove from the oven, sprinkle with coriander and serve hot.

Serves 6.

QUESADILLAS

12 Corn Tortillas
315 ml (10 fl oz/1 ¼ cups) thick sour cream
185 g (6 oz) Cheddar cheese, grated
1 small onion, very finely chopped
1 teaspoon chilli powder
1 fresh green chilli, finely chopped
1 tablespoon finely chopped fresh coriander

Separately heat tortillas in a hot, dry frying pan for 30 seconds. Place a tablespoon of sour cream on one half of a tortilla, top with grated cheese, then onion, sprinkle with chilli powder, chilli and coriander. Fold over the other half of the tortilla and secure with a wooden cocktail stick. Repeat with remaining tortillas.

Heat a frying pan until a few drops of water sizzle when sprinkled on it. Cook one quesadilla at a time, one side for 45 seconds, turn over and cook another 45 seconds. Repeat once more so the cheese melts. Serve immediately.

Serves 6.

Note: Quesadillas may also be placed on a baking tray, covered with foil, and baked on the top shelf of a heated oven at 190°C (375°F/Gas 5) for 15 minutes.

TORTILLAS WITH CREAM & CHEESE

100 ml (3 ¹/₂ fl oz/¹/₃ cup) sunflower oil
1 medium onion, finely chopped
1 clove garlic, finely chopped
500 g (1 lb) tomatoes, blanched, skinned, seeded
    and mashed to pulp
1 teaspoon finely chopped fresh coriander
salt and pepper
12 Wheat Tortillas, cut into 2.5 cm (1 in) wide strips
    (1 in) wide strips
250 ml (8 fl oz/1 cup) double (thick) cream
90 g (3 oz) Parmesan cheese, grated

Pre-heat the oven to 190°C (375°F/Gas 5).
Grease a 1.1 litre (2 pint) ovenproof dish.

Heat 2 tablespoons oil in a saucepan over
medium heat. Fry the onion and garlic
gently for about 5 minutes until soft but not
brown. Add the tomatoes and coriander
and season with salt and pepper. Simmer
for about 10 minutes, until reduced.

Heat the remaining oil in a frying pan over
medium heat and fry the tortilla strips for 45
seconds each side, without browning. Drain
on absorbent kitchen paper. Pour half the
tomato mixture into the dish. Top with
tortilla strips, then the cream, and finish
with the remaining sauce. Sprinkle with the
cheese. Bake for 20 minutes.

Serves 6.

TUNA CASSEROLE

1 tablespoon oil
1 medium onion, chopped
1 clove garlic, crushed in ½ teaspoon salt
500 g (1 lb) tomatoes, blanched, peeled, chopped
1 tablespoon tomato purée (paste)
8 black olives, stoned and sliced
1 green chilli, seeded and chopped
½ green pepper (capsicum), seeded and chopped
1 teaspoon ground cumin
200 g (7 oz) can tuna, drained
185 g (6 oz) cottage cheese
1 egg
185 g (6 oz) Cheddar cheese, grated
4 Corn or Wheat Tortillas, cut into strips
    into strips

Pre-heat the oven to 180°C (350°F/Gas 4).

Heat the oil in a medium saucepan, add the
garlic and onion and fry gently until soft
but not brown. Add tomatoes, tomato purée
(paste), olives, chilli, green pepper (capsicum)
and cumin. Bring to the boil, cover, then simmer for 15 minutes until fairly thick; remove
the lid if necessary. Add the tuna and carefully
stir well.

Mix the cottage cheese with the egg. Place
half the tomato mixture in a shallow
ovenproof dish. Cover with half the grated
cheese. Spread the cottage cheese mixture
over the top, then cover with the tortilla
strips. Spoon over the remaining tomato
mixture. Sprinkle with the remaining grated
cheese. Bake for 30 minutes until bubbling
and golden brown.

Serves 4.

CRAB ENCHILADAS

3 tablespoons sunflower oil
12 Wheat or Corn Tortillas
1 quantity Cooked Tomato Sauce
155 ml (5 fl oz/²/₃ cup) sour cream
1 tablespoon chopped fresh coriander to garnish
30 g (1 oz) toasted slivered almonds to garnish

Filling:
1 tablespoon olive oil
1 small onion, finely chopped
1 small clove garlic, finely chopped
185 g (6 oz) cooked or drained canned crab, or
**   thawed if frozen, flaked**
3 green olives, stoned and chopped
30 g (1 oz /¹/₄ cup) raisins, soaked in hot water for
at least 2 hours, drained
30 g (1 oz/¹/₄ cup) chopped almonds
1 tablespoon chopped fresh coriander
1 teaspoon capers
salt

To make filling, heat oil in a medium saucepan, add onion and garlic and cook gently until soft but not brown, 5-10 minutes. Stir in remaining ingredients. Heat gently for 3-5 minutes. Keep warm.

Pre-heat the oven to 180°C (350°F/Gas 4). Grease a shallow ovenproof dish. Heat the oil in a large, heavy frying pan. Using tongs, carefully place one tortilla at a time in hot oil. Hold for 3-5 seconds until softened. Quickly turn tortilla and repeat on second side. Drain on absorbent kitchen paper.

In a saucepan over low heat, warm Cooked Tomato Sauce, stirring occasionally. Spoon filling onto each tortilla, roll up, and place seamside down in the ovenproof dish.

Pour Tomato Sauce over the enchiladas, cover with foil and bake for 15 minutes to heat through.

Pour the sour cream in a small saucepan and heat gently. Pour over the enchiladas and sprinkle with coriander and toasted almonds.

Serves 6.

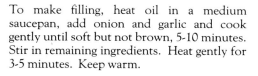

BAKED SPICED FISH

¼ green pepper, seeded and chopped
¼ red pepper, seeded and chopped
2 tablespoons chopped coriander leaves
1 teaspoon ground cumin
½ teaspoon chilli powder
1 clove garlic, crushed
1 tablespoon white wine vinegar
salt
1 kg (2 lb) whole sea bream, cleaned
1 oz (2 tablespoons) butter
about 315 ml (10 fl oz/1¼ cups) milk
3 tablespoons cornflour (cornstarch)

Pre-heat oven to 180°C (350°F/Gas 4).

In a bowl mix the peppers (capsicums), coriander, cumin, chilli powder, garlic, vinegar and salt. Place fish on a large sheet of foil that will enclose it completely; place on a baking sheet. Stuff the fish with pepper (capsicum) mixture, spreading any remaining over top. Dot with butter. Fold foil over fish and seal edges tightly. Bake for 25 minutes until the fish flakes easily with the back of a knife. Carefully unwrap fish and transfer to a warmed plate; reserve baking juices. Cover fish and keep warm.

Strain baking juices into a measuring jug. Make up to 440ml (14 fl oz/1¹/₃ cups) with milk. In a saucepan, mix cornflour (cornstarch) with a little of the liquid to make a paste, then gradually stir in remaining liquid. Bring to the boil, stirring with a wooden spoon. Simmer for 1 minute. Adjust seasoning if necessary. Pour into a warmed sauceboat and serve with the fish.

Serves 6.

FISH IN GREEN SAUCE

500 g (1 lb) tomatillos or green tomatoes
3 spring onions, trimmed and chopped
1 tablespoon chopped fresh coriander
1 clove garlic
4 tablespoons sunflower oil
1 small green chilli
salt
500 g (1 lb) haddock fillets or white fish fillets
3 tablespoons fresh lime juice

Discard the paper husks from the tomatillos and rinse. If using green tomatoes, blanch and remove the skins.

Pour cold water into a medium saucepan until 1 cm (½ in) deep. Place the tomatillos or green tomatoes in the pan. Bring to the boil, then reduce heat and simmer, covered for 10 minutes or until tender. Drain and cool. Place the tomatillos or green tomatoes in a blender or food processor with the spring onions, coriander, garlic and chilli, and process until smooth.

Heat 1 tablespoon oil in a pan. Add the tomatillos, or green tomato mixture, and season with salt. Bring to the boil, reduce the heat and simmer, uncovered, for 15 minutes. Keep warm. Sprinkle fish with the lime juice, then with salt. Leave for 5 minutes. Heat remaining oil in a large frying pan. Add fish and cook for 1 minute on each side. Pour sauce over the fish, cover and simmer for 5 minutes, or until the fish flakes easily with the back of a knife.

Serves 4.

HOT FISH BURRITOS

12 Wheat Tortillas
90 g (3 oz) grated Cheddar cheese, Guacamole, shredded lettuce and tomato to serve

Filling:
375 g (12 oz) cod fillets, or other firm white fish
1 tablespoon olive oil
1 small onion, finely chopped
1 green chilli, finely chopped
½ teaspoon chilli powder
155 ml (5 fl oz / ²/₃ cup) thick sour cream
1 tablespoon finely chopped fresh coriander
salt and pepper

Pre-heat oven to 180°C (350°F/Gas 4). Grease a large, shallow ovenproof dish.

Rinse the fish with cold water and pat dry with absorbent kitchen paper. Put the fish in a large frying pan. Just cover with water, and season with salt and pepper. Bring to the boil, then reduce the heat so the liquid barely moves. Cover and poach for 5-7 minutes or until the fish flakes easily when tested with the back of a knife.

Drain the fish; discard the liquid. Flake fish, carefully removing any bones and skin. Put fish into a bowl. Heat the oil in a small frying pan and gently fry the onion and chillies until soft. Drain off the excess oil, and add the onion and chillies to the fish. Add sour cream and coriander and season with salt and pepper; mix well.

Warm each tortilla in a dry hot frying pan for 40 seconds until pliable. Remove from pan.

Fold 2 sides of one tortilla into the centre, overlapping the edges a little. Fold the part nearest you towards the centre, forming a pocket; fill pocket with fish mixture. Secure with a wooden cocktail stick then place the burrito in the ovenproof dish. Repeat until all the burritos are filled.

Sprinkle with cheese, cover with foil, and bake for 30 minutes. Discard the cocktail sticks. Serve with Guacamole, shredded lettuce and tomato.

Serves 6.

RED SNAPPER VERACRUZ-STYLE

— FISH IN GARLIC SAUCE —

2 tablespoons olive oil
1 medium onion, chopped
3 cloves garlic, peeled and very finely chopped
500 g (1lb) tomatoes, peeled and chopped
10 green olives, stoned and chopped
2 tablespoons capers
3 bay leaves
6 black peppercorns
salt
1 kg (2 lb) red snapper, or other white fish fillets

500 g (1 lb) haddock or sole fillets
juice of 1 small lime
salt and pepper
3 tablespoons olive oil
3 garlic cloves, peeled and chopped
3 tablespoons sunflower oil
1 tablespoon chopped coriander

Wipe the fish with damp absorbent kitchen paper. Pour over lime juice and sprinkle with salt and pepper. Leave to stand for at least 30 minutes.

Heat oil in a large saucepan. Add onion and garlic and fry gently for 5-10 minutes until soft but not brown. Add tomatoes, olives, capers, bay leaves, peppercorns and salt. Bring to the boil, then reduce the heat and simmer, uncovered, for 10 minutes.

Heat the olive oil in a small saucepan, over a medium heat. Add the garlic and cook for about 5 minutes until a light golden brown. Keep warm. Meanwhile, heat the sunflower oil in a large frying pan. Add the fish fillets and fry gently until the fish flakes easily when tested with the back of a knife, about 5-7 minutes, turning once.

Place fish in a large frying pan and sprinkle with salt. Pour over tomato mixture. Bring slowly to the boil, reduce the heat, cover and simmer for about 7 minutes until fish flakes easily when tested with the back of a knife.

Serves 6.

Divide the fish between four warmed plates. Spoon the garlic and oil over each serving. Sprinkle with coriander and serve.

Serves 4.

COD YUCATAN-STYLE

4 fresh cod cutlets, 125-185 g (4-6 oz) each
2 tablespoons fresh lime juice
salt and pepper
1 tablespoon olive oil
1 small onion, finely chopped
1 small green pepper (capsicum), seeded and
    chopped
60 g (2 oz) pumpkin seeds
2 tablespoons finely chopped coriander
60 ml (2 fl oz/ ¼ cup) orange juice
2 hard-boiled eggs, quartered, and lime wedges to
    garnish

Pre-heat oven to 180°C (350°F/Gas 4).

Wipe the fish with absorbent kitchen paper. Rub the lime juice into the fish. Place cutlets in shallow ovenproof dish. Season lightly with salt and pepper. Heat oil in a medium saucepan. Add the onion, green pepper (capsicum), pumpkin seeds, and half the coriander. Fry gently until the onion is soft, but not brown 5-10 minutes.

Place in the cavities in the cutlets and spread the remainder over the top. Pour over orange juice. Cover and bake for 15-20 minutes or until the fish flakes easily with the back of a knife. Garnish with egg quarters and lime wedges.

Serves 4.

CHILLI FISH

30 g (1 oz / 2 tablespoons) butter
1 teaspoon hot chilli powder
2 medium onions, finely chopped
1 clove garlic crushed in ¼ teaspon salt
625 ml (20 fl oz / 2 ½ cups) chicken stock
2 tablespoons tomato purée (paste)
juice of 1 lemon
2 teaspoons clear honey
500 g (1 lb) cod or haddock fillet, cut into 2.5 cm
    (1 in) pieces
salt and pepper

Melt butter in a saucepan. Add chilli powder and cook over a low heat for 1 minute. Add the onions and garlic and fry for 3 minutes. Stir in stock, tomato purée (paste), lemon juice and honey. Cover, and simmer for 30 minutes, until quite thick.

Add the fish and simmer for 10 minutes. Season with salt and pepper.

Serves 4.

Variation: Substitute 250 g (8 oz) peeled cooked prawns for 250 g (8 oz) of the fish; add the prawns half-way through the cooking.

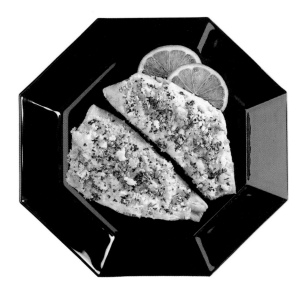

RED SNAPPER IN CORIANDER

1 kg (2lb) red snapper, or other firm white fish
    fillets
60 ml (2 fl oz / ¼ cup) fresh lime juice
salt
60 ml (2 fl oz / ¼ cup) olive oil
30 g (1 oz) fresh white breadcrumbs
1 clove garlic, finely chopped
6 tablespoons chopped fresh coriander
1 teaspoon grated lime rind
pepper

Rinse and dry the fish fillets. Lightly oil a heavy frying pan. Rub the fish with half the lime juice and 1 teaspoon salt and place in the pan, skin-side down.

Add enough cold water to cover. Bring to the boil then reduce the heat and simmer for 5 minutes, turning once. In another pan, heat half the oil, then add breadcrumbs, garlic, salt and 4 tablespoons coriander. Cook over a low heat, stirring constantly until the crumbs are browned. Spread over the fish. Simmer for 5 minutes or until the fish flakes easily when tested with the back of a knife.

Mix the remaining lime juice and oil together and pour over the fish. Cook for 2-3 minutes. Combine remaining coriander and grated lime rind and pepper and sprinkle over the fish.

Serves 4-6.

MEXICALI CHICKEN

2 tablespoons sunflower oil
1 medium sized onion, chopped
1 small fresh green chilli, seeded and chopped
1 clove garlic, finely chopped
2 tablespoons tomato purée (paste)
1 teaspoon ground cumin
1 tablespoon finely chopped fresh coriander
250 g (8 oz) cooked red kidney beans
500 g (1 lb) tomatoes, blanched, skinned, chopped
500 g (1 lb) cooked chicken
salt and pepper
boiled rice or Corn or Wheat Tortillas and a green salad to serve

Heat oil in a heavy saucepan and fry over medium heat the onion, chilli and garlic for 4-5 minutes until the onion is soft but not brown.

Stir in tomato purée (paste), cumin, coriander, beans, tomatoes and chicken; season with salt and pepper. Cover and simmer for 20 minutes until thick; if necessary, uncover and simmer for a further 10 minutes. Serve with boiled rice or Tortillas and a salad.

Serves 4.

MOLE POBLANO

approximately 125 ml (4 fl oz / ½ cup) sunflower oil
one 4 kg (8 lb) turkey, cut into serving portions
1 large onion, chopped
2 cloves garlic, finely chopped

Sauce:
6 ancho chillies, seeded and chopped
6 mulata chillies, seeded and chopped
4 pastilla chillies, seeded and chopped
500 ml (16 fl oz / 2½ cups) warm water
125 g (4 oz / 1 cup) blanched slivered almonds
60 g (2 oz / ⅓ cup) roasted peanuts
4 tablespoons sesame seeds
½ teaspoon coriander seeds
¼ teaspoon aniseed
2 cloves
1 cm (½ in) piece cinnamon stick
2 medium sized onions, chopped
2 garlic cloves, finely chopped
500 g (1 lb) tomatoes, skinned, seeded and chopped
90 g (3 oz / ⅓ cup) seedless raisins
2 Corn or Wheat Tortillas, recipe page 13/14, cut
  into small pieces
45 g (1½ oz) plain (dark) chocolate, broken
salt
boiled rice, Basic Beans and Salad to serve.

Heat 2 tablespoons oil in a large heavy frying pan and fry turkey pieces, a few at a time, until browned all over, add more oil as necessary. Transfer turkey to a large heavy flameproof casserole or saucepan. Add onion, garlic and enough water to cover. Simmer for 1 hour until turkey is tender. Using a slotted spoon, remove turkey, cover and keep warm. Strain and reserve the stock. Rinse and dry casserole.

Put chillies in a bowl with the warm water, leave for 30 minutes, stirring occasionally. In a blender or food processor, process almonds, peanuts, half the sesame seeds, all the coriander seeds, aniseed, cloves and cinnamon. Transfer to a bowl.

In a blender or food processor, combine chillies and the water, onions, garlic, tomatoes, raisins and tortillas. Process to a thick paste, this may have to be done in two batches. Transfer to a bowl and stir in ground nuts and spices. Measure oil left in frying pan and make up to 60 ml (2 fl oz / ¼ cup). Put pan over a medium heat, add paste mixture and fry, stirring. Transfer to the casserole. Stir in 500 ml (16 fl oz / 2 cups) reserved turkey stock, and chocolate. Season with salt and simmer until chocolate has melted and the sauce has the consistency of double (thick) cream.

Cover and simmer gently, stirring occasionally for 20 minutes. Add turkey pieces to sauce, turning them to coat well. Cover and simmer a further 10 minutes. Arrange turkey in a large, deep, warmed serving dish, and pour over sauce. In a small frying pan over low heat, toast remaining sesame seeds and sprinkle over turkey. Serve with rice, Beans, and Christmas Salad.

Serves 10.

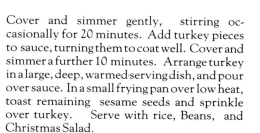

CARNITAS

1 onion, chopped
3 cloves garlic
3 tablespoons malt vinegar
salt and pepper
pinch of granulated sugar
1.5 kg (3 lb) shoulder of pork
625 ml (20 fl oz/2½ cups) water
250 g (8 oz) lard, diced
warm Corn or Wheat Tortillas to serve

Put the onion, garlic, vinegar, salt, pepper and sugar in a blender or food processor and process until smooth. Transfer to a bowl.

Remove the bone from meat; reserve the bone. Cut the meat into large chunks, add to the onion mixture and stir to well coat. Put into flameproof dish, cover and refrigerate overnight. Pre-heat oven to 160°C (325°F/Gas 3). Add the water, reserved bone and lard to casserole dish. Cover and place in the oven for 2 hours, basting and turning occasionally.

Using a slotted spoon, lift the meat from the casserole, and put into a roasting tin. Put roasting tin in the oven for 30 minutes or until meat is golden brown. Meanwhile, skim all the fat from the liquid in the casserole; discard the bone. Boil the liquid rapidly until reduced to 90 ml (3 fl oz /¹/₃ cup). Transfer the meat to a warmed serving dish and pour the sauce over. Serve with warm Tortillas.

Serves 6.

MEXICAN PORK CHOPS

2 cloves garlic, peeled and halved
4 pork chops
2 tablespoons oil
1 medium avocado pear to garnish
1 tablespoon lemon juice

Sauce:
3 fresh green chillies, finely chopped
750 g (1½ lb) tomatoes, blanched, skinned, chopped
2 small onions, chopped
1 clove garlic salt

Rub the garlic over the chops; cover and leave in refrigerator for 5 hours. To make the sauce put the chillies in a saucepan, cover with water, and bring to the boil; cook for 3 minutes. Drain. Remove the stems and cut chillies in half lengthways. Discard white pith and seeds. Put chillies in a blender or food processor, add the tomatoes, onions, garlic and salt and process until smooth; set aside.

Heat the oil in a frying pan. Fry the chops for 5 minutes on each side or until brown. Pour over the chilli mixture and simmer, uncovered, for 15 minutes. Peel the avocado. Cut in half and remove the stone. Slice and sprinkle with lemon juice. Put chops on a warmed serving plate, spoon over sauce and garnish with avocado slices.

Serves 4.

EMPANADAS

Pastry:
185 g (6 oz / 1½ cups) self-raising flour
60 g (2 oz / ¼ cup) unsalted butter, diced and chilled
60 g (2 oz/ ¼ cup) lard, diced and chilled
1 tablespoon lemon juice
90 ml (3 fl oz / ⅓ cup) cold water
beaten egg to glaze

Filling:
1 quantity Picadillo
½ quantity Cooked Tomato Sauce
½ quantity Re-fried Beans

Pre-heat oven to 220°C (425F/Gas 7). Lightly grease a baking tray.

On a lightly floured surface, using a floured rolling pin, roll out pastry to 3 mm (1/8 in) thick. Cut out eight circles 15 cm (6 in) in diameter. On one half of each circle put a spoonful of Picadillo, a spoonful of Tomato Sauce, then a spoonful of Re-fried Beans.

For the pastry, sift the flour into a mixing bowl. Toss in butter and lard. Using a knife, carefully stir in lemon juice and sufficient water to make a soft dough. Place on a lightly floured surface. Using a floured rolling pin, roll out to a rectangle 2.5 cm (1 in) thick. Lightly mark pastry crossways into thirds. Fold up lowest third over dough; seal, fold top third down over dough. Seal edges with a rolling pin. Give pastry a quarter turn. Repeat rolling, folding and turning 3 times.

Dampen edges with cold water. Fold pastry over filling; seal edges well, brush with egg and place on the baking tray, spaced well apart. Bake for about 20 minutes or until golden brown and well risen.

Serve hot or cold.

Serves 8.

Put pastry in a plastic bag and refrigerate 1 hour.

PORK COASTAL-STYLE

2 tablespoons oil
1 kg (2 lb) pork fillet, cut into 2.5 cm (1 in) cubes
90 g (3 oz / $^3/_4$ cup) seasoned flour
1 large onion, chopped
500 ml (16 fl oz / 2 cups) beef stock
1 teaspoon ground coriander
1 clove garlic, finely chopped
1 fresh green chilli, seeded and chopped
2 tomatoes, blanched, skinned and chopped
1 red pepper (capsicum), seeded and chopped
$^1/_2$ fresh pineapple, peeled, cored and cut into chunks
2 medium sweet potatoes, peeled and diced
1 tablespoon finely chopped fresh coriander to garnish

Pre-heat oven 180°C (350°F/Gas4). Heat the oil in a large, heavy frying pan. Toss pork in flour and fry until evenly brown, turning frequently. Transfer meat to a large, flameproof casserole. Add onion to frying pan and fry gently until soft; add a little more oil if necessary. Stir in stock and bring to the boil, stirring. Add ground coriander, garlic, chilli, tomatoes and pepper (capsicum). Simmer for 5 minutes. Pour over the pork.

Bring to the boil, cover and bake for 1 ½ – 2 hours until tender. Add pineapple and sweet potatoes. Return to the oven and bake for a further 20-25 minutes until the fruit and vegetables are tender. Garnish with coriander.

Serves 6.

CHICKEN ENCHILADAS

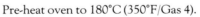

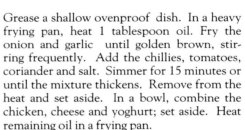

60 ml (2 fl oz / ¼ cup) oil
1 medium onion, finely chopped
1 clove garlic, finely chopped
4 fresh green chillies, seeded and finely chopped
3 tomatoes, skinned and chopped
1 tablespoon finely chopped fresh coriander
salt
250 g (8 oz) cooked chicken, shredded
125 g (4 oz) *queso fresco*, Wensleydale, Cheshire or Lancashire cheese, grated
315 ml (10 fl oz/1 ¼ cups) natural yoghurt
12 Wheat Tortillas

Pre-heat oven to 180°C (350°F/Gas 4).

Grease a shallow ovenproof dish. In a heavy frying pan, heat 1 tablespoon oil. Fry the onion and garlic until golden brown, stirring frequently. Add the chillies, tomatoes, coriander and salt. Simmer for 15 minutes or until the mixture thickens. Remove from the heat and set aside. In a bowl, combine the chicken, cheese and yoghurt; set aside. Heat remaining oil in a frying pan.

Using tongs, place one tortilla in the oil for 3-5 seconds until softened. Repeat on the other side, then drain on absorbent kitchen paper. Fill each tortilla with chicken mixture and roll up. Arrange seam-side down and close together in the ovenproof dish. Pour over the tomato mixture and cover the dish with foil. Bake 20 minutes until heated through.

Serves 6.

— MEATBALLS IN HOT SAUCE —

Meatballs:
1 kg (2 lb) minced pork
1 large onion, finely chopped
2 cloves garlic, finely chopped
60 g (2 oz/½ cup) ground almonds
60 g (2 oz/1 cup) fresh breadcrumbs
1 egg, lightly beaten
1 tablespoon finely chopped fresh coriander
¾ teaspoon ground cinnamon
3 tablespoons dry sherry
salt and pepper
30 g (1 oz/2 tablespoons) butter
2 tablespoons olive oil

Sauce:
1 tablespoon sunflower oil
1 large onion, finely chopped
1 clove garlic, crushed
1 teaspoon soft brown sugar
6 medium tomatoes, skinned and chopped
1 medium green pepper (capsicum), seeded and sliced
1 medium red pepper (capsicum), seeded and sliced
1 fresh green chilli, finely chopped
¾ teaspoon cayenne pepper
1 teaspoon paprika
1 tablespoon finely chopped coriander
75 ml (2 ¾ fl oz/⅓ cup) beef stock
2 teaspoons cornflour (cornstarch)
60 ml (2 fl oz/¼ cup) dry sherry
salt and pepper

For the meatballs, in a large bowl mix together the pork, onion, garlic, almonds, breadcrumbs, egg, coriander, cinnamon, sherry, salt and pepper. Using wet hands, form mixture into 36 meatballs.

Melt the butter and oil in a frying pan and fry the meatballs a few at a time for 5 minutes until well browned. Drain on absorbent kitchen paper. Keep warm.

To make the sauce, put oil, onion, garlic and sugar in a saucepan. Fry very gently for 6-8 minutes. Add the tomatoes, peppers (capsicums), chilli, cayenne pepper, paprika and coriander. Simmer for 3 minutes. Add the stock.

In a small bowl, mix to a paste the cornflour (cornstarch) and sherry; stir into the pan. Bring to the boil, stirring, then reduce the heat and simmer for 2 minutes; season with salt and pepper. Add meatballs and simmer for 20-25 minutes or until the sauce is fairly thick.

Serves 6.

RUM-BARBECUED STEAK

155 ml (5 fl oz / ^{2}/$_3$ cup) rum
2 cloves garlic, crushed
1 teaspoon chilli powder
1 tablespoon finely chopped fresh coriander
^{1}/$_2$ teaspoon Tabasco sauce
1 kg (2 lb) piece rump or sirloin steak, 5 cm (2 in) thick
Mexican Rice, Re-fried Beans and a salad to serve

Mix together rum, garlic, chilli powder, coriander and Tabasco sauce.

Rinse steak under cold water and dry. Place in a shallow, ovenproof dish and pour over rum mixture. Cover, and leave for at least 30 minutes, but preferably in a refrigerator over night. Heat barbecue, or pre-heat grill to highest temperature. Remove steak from dish; reserve marinade.

Place steak over a hot barbecue or under a very hot grill and cook for 5 minutes a side, or longer if desired, turning occasionally and basting frequently with marinade. Carve steak into thin slices. Serve with Mexacan Rice, Re-fried Beans, and a salad.

Serves 4.

Note: If steak has been in refrigerator overnight, transfer to room temperature 45 minutes before cooking.

CHILLI CON CARNE

2 tablespoons oil
30 g (1 oz / 2 tablespoons) plain (all purpose) flour
salt and pepper
500 g (1 lb) stewing steak, cut into 2.5 cm (1 in) cubes
1 bay leaf
1 large onion, chopped
1 clove garlic, finely chopped
2 teaspoons hot chilli powder
500 g (1 lb) tomatoes, skinned, chopped
2 tablespoons tomato purée (paste)
^{1}/$_4$ quantity Basic Beans

Pre-heat oven 160°C (325°F/Gas 3).

In a large frying pan, heat the oil. Season flour with salt and pepper. Toss the meat in seasoned flour and fry until evenly browned; add more oil if necessary to prevent sticking. Using a slotted spoon remove the meat, drain on absorbent kitchen paper then put into an ovenproof casserole. Add bay leaf. Add the onion and garlic to frying pan and fry gently for 5 minutes. Stir in chilli powder, tomatoes and tomato purée (paste).

Pour into casserole. Cover and cook in oven for 1 hour 20 minutes until meat is tender. Remove from oven, and stir in beans. Cover, return to oven, and cook for a further 15 minutes.

Serves 6-8.

GRILLED STEAK

625 g (1 lb 4 oz) piece sirloin steak
2 tablespoons sunflower oil
1 tablespoon chopped fresh coriander
salt and pepper
75 ml (2 ^{1}/$_2$ fl oz / ^{1}/$_3$ cup) fresh orange juice
1 tablespoon fresh lime juice
2 teaspoons cider vinegar
orange slices to garnish

Wipe meat with damp absorbent kitchen paper. Put in a shallow dish. Put the oil, coriander, salt, pepper, orange juice, lime juice and vinegar in a bowl and mix well. Pour over steak, cover and leave in refrigerator overnight.

Transfer to room temperature 45 minutes before cooking. Pre-heat grill to the highest temperature. Lift steak from marinade, allowing excess to drain off; reserve marinade. Place steak on grill rack. Grill for 5 minutes each side, or longer is desired, basting with the marinade. Cook for a little longer if a more well-cooked meat is preferred. Garnish with orange slices.

Serves 4.

LAMB WITH RED WINE

3 fresh green chillies, seeded and finely chopped
315 ml (10 fl oz / 1 ¼ cups) red wine
2 cloves garlic
2 thin slices fresh ginger, peeled
1 teaspoon ground cumin
1 tablespoon finely chopped fresh coriander
salt
8 small lamb loin chops, 1 kg (2 lb) total weight

Put chillies, wine, garlic, ginger, cumin, coriander and salt in a blender or food processor, and process to a purée. Press through a sieve.

Wipe lamb with damp absorbent kitchen paper. Place in a large, shallow, ovenproof dish. Pour chilli mixture over, cover and place in refrigerator for 8 hours, turning occasionally. Pre-heat oven to 180°C (350°F/Gas 4). Cover the dish with foil and bake for 1 hour, or until the chops are very tender.

Serves 4.

– CHORIZO & CHEESE PANCAKES –

250 g (8 oz) chorizo, chopped
185 g (6 oz) Cheddar cheese, grated

Pancakes:
125 g (4 oz/1 cup) plain (all purpose) flour, sifted
2 eggs
155 ml (5 fl oz/²/₃ cup) milk
5 tablespoons water
salt
approximately 60 g (2 oz/4 tablespoons) melted
    butter, for cooking pancakes

Sauce:
2 tablespoons oil
1 small onion, finely chopped
1 clove garlic, finely chopped
2 large tomatoes, skinned and chopped
3 tablespoons tomato purée (paste)
1 bay leaf
salt and pepper
1 fresh green chilli, seeded and chopped
75 ml (2 ½ fl oz/¹/₃ cup) thick sour cream
1 tablespoon finely chopped fresh coriander

To make the pancakes, put flour, eggs, milk, water and salt into a blender or food processor. Mix for 1 minute at high speed. Scrape down the sides of blender or processor with a spatula and blend again for 15 seconds until smooth.

Heat butter in a 15 cm (6 in) heavy frying pan over medium heat. Pour in batter to coat base thinly. Quickly tilt pan in all directions to allow batter to coat the bottom evenly. Cook for 1 minute, then, using a spatula, turn over pancake. Cook 30-60 seconds until set and speckled brown. Slide onto a warmed plate and cover with a tea towel. Repeat until batter is used.

Pre-heat oven to 180°C (350°F/Gas 4). Grease a shallow ovenproof dish.

To make the sauce, heat the oil in a saucepan and gently fry onion and garlic for about 5 minutes until soft. Add the tomatoes, tomato purée (paste), bay leaf, salt and pepper. Simmer for 15 minutes. Discard the bay leaf. Pour into a blender or food processor with the chilli and sour cream and process until smooth. Mix in the coriander.

Pour half the tomato sauce into the dish. Divide the chorizo and half the cheese evenly among the pancakes. Roll up tightly and place seam-side down in dish. Pour over the remaining sauce and sprinkle with the remaining cheese. Bake for 15-20 minutes.

Serves 6.

HOT CHILLI SAUCE

1 clove garlic
1 teaspoon chilli powder
1 jalapeño chilli
2 dried red chillies
1 fresh green chilli
155 ml (5 fl oz / ²/3 cup) water
155 ml (5 fl oz / ²/3 cup) thick sour cream
salt and pepper

Place all the ingredients except the salt and pepper in a blender or food processor and process until smooth. Season.

Transfer to a small serving bowl. Serve as a relish.

Makes 310 ml (10 fl oz / 2 ¼ cups).

Note: Keep for up to 24 hours in a covered container in the refrigerator.

SALSA FRESCA

4 large, ripe, firm tomatoes, roughly chopped
1 tablespoon finely chopped fresh coriander
½ small onion, finely chopped
2 fresh green chillies, finely chopped
juice of ½ lemon
½ teaspoon salt
1 teaspoon freshly ground black pepper

Mix all the ingredients together and leave for 15 minutes before serving. Serve as an accompaniment to any bean, rice or meat dish.

Makes 315 ml (10 fl oz / 1 ¼ cups).

Note: The relish does not keep long, so if there is any left, fry it in a little oil and serve as a sauce for enchilada recipes, or over Ranch-Style Eggs for breakfast.

GREEN CHILLI RELISH

1 clove garlic, crushed in ½ teaspoon salt
1 small onion, very finely chopped
6 green or red tomatoes, peeled, seeded and finely chopped
6 green chillies, seeded and very finely chopped
2 tablespoons oil
1 tablespoon white wine vinegar

In a medium bowl, combine garlic, onion, tomatoes and chillies. In a small bowl, stir together the salt, pepper, oil and vinegar.

Pour onto the tomato and chilli mixture. Stir well. Transfer to a serving bowl.

Makes 155 ml (5 fl oz / 2/3 cup).

Note: Keep for up to 24 hours in a covered container in refrigerator.

ALMOND SAUCE

30 ml (1 fl oz / 2 tablespoons) sunflower oil
½ small onion, very finely chopped
1 small clove garlic
30 g (1 oz / 2 tablespoons) sugar
2 tablespoons vinegar
3 tablespoons tomato purée (paste)
60 g (2 oz / ½ cup) ground almonds
salt and pepper

Heat the oil in a medium saucepan. Add the garlic and onion and cook gently, stirring occasionally, until soft but not brown. Add the sugar, vinegar, tomato purée (paste) and ground almonds.

Bring slowly to the boil, stirring constantly, then reduce the heat and simmer gently for 2 minutes. Season with salt and pepper. Serve hot with fish or chicken.

Serves 4.

SALSA VERDE

SALAD DRESSING

500 g (1 lb) tomatillos, skinned and roughly chopped
½ onion, finely chopped
1 tablespoon finely chopped fresh coriander
salt and pepper

3 tablespoons sunflower oil
1 tablespoon vinegar
¼ teaspoon French mustard
salt and pepper
1 tablespoon finely chopped fresh coriander

Put all the ingredients in a bowl and mix together well. For a smoother consistency, put all the ingredients in a blender or food processor and process until smooth.

Put all the ingredients in a screw-topped jar. Shake hard until well-blended. Store, in the jar, in the refrigerator for up to three days.

Shake well before serving.

Serves 4.

Use as a garnish for tacos or as an accompaniment to a meal.

Makes 500 ml (16 fl oz / 2 cups).

CHAYOTE SALAD

1 kg (2 lb) chayote
90 ml (3 fl oz / 1/3 cup) olive oil
2 teaspoons finely chopped fresh coriander
2 tablespoons white wine vinegar
salt and pepper
1 avocado pear, peeled, stoned, cut into strips
100 g (3 1/2 oz) Mozzarella cheese, cut into strips
8 green olives, sliced

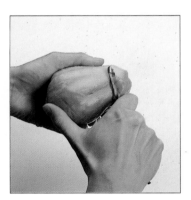

Peel chayote, halve and remove the stone; chop the flesh. Steam the flesh over boiling, salted water about 20 minutes until tender. Cool. In a screwtop jar, shake together olive oil, coriander, vinegar, salt and pepper.

Peel avocado. Slice flesh into a serving bowl and immediately toss with the olive oil dressing. Toss in chayote and scatter over cheese and olives.

Serves 4-6.

CHRISTMAS SALAD

1 Cos lettuce
2 small cooked beetroot, sliced
1 large carrot, finely diced
1 cooking apple
fresh lemon juice
1/4 fresh pineapple, peeled, cored and diced
1 banana

Dressing:
1 tablespoon lemon juice
3 tablespoons sunflower oil
salt and pepper
60 g (2 oz / 1/2 cup) toasted slivered almonds to garnish
1 orange, peeled, segmented and chopped to garnish

Use half the lettuce leaves to line base and sides of a shallow serving dish. Arrange beetroot on lettuce. Shred remaining lettuce and put in a bowl. Peel, core and dice apple. Add carrot and pineapple. Slice the banana, sprinkle with lemon juice. Add to the bowl.

Put lemon juice, oil and salt in a screw-top jar and shake well. Pour over the fruit and carrot. Toss gently. Pile the mixture over the beetroot. Garnish with almonds and oranges.

Serves 6.

TOMATO SALAD

1 large, ripe avocado pear
1 teaspoon olive oil
1 teaspoon lemon juice
30 g (1 oz) cooked ham, diced
salt and pepper
4 large lettuce leaves
4 medium tomatoes, thinly sliced
4 springs of fresh coriander to garnish

Cut the avocado in half, remove the stone, and scoop the flesh into a bowl. Add the oil, lemon juice and ham and season with salt and pepper; mix well.

Line a serving dish with the lettuce leaves. Arrange tomatoes on top, followed by avocado mixture. Garnish with coriander.

Serves 4.

SPRING ONION SALAD

8 spring onions, cut in 1 cm (½ in) slices
125 g (4 oz) courgettes (zucchini), cut in 2.5 cm
    (1 in) slices
1 large green pepper (capsicum), cut into strips
3 medium tomatoes, skinned, seeded and chopped
3 tablespoons olive oil
1 tablespoon white wine vinegar
salt and pepper
1 tablespoon chopped fresh coriander

Boil the spring onions just covered by salted water for 3 minutes until just tender. Drain. Put into a serving bowl. Boil courgettes (zucchini) just covered by salted water for 5 minutes. Drain. Add to spring onions with the pepper (capsicum) and tomatoes.

Put the oil, vinegar, salt and pepper into a screw-top jar. Shake well and pour over the vegetables. Toss gently, then cover and chill. Toss again just before serving, and garnish with coriander.

Serves 4.

TACO SHELL SALAD

sunflower oil for deep frying
twelve Corn Tortillas

Filling:
½ crisp lettuce, shredded
1 quantity Picadillo
1 large onion, finely chopped
6 large tomatoes, skinned, finely chopped

Heat oil in a deep-fat frying pan to 180°C (350°F).

Fry tortillas by holding two at a time with tongs, and pressing them against the side of the pan to make a U-shape. Hold in position for 1 minute, then separate the two tortillas and fry for about 3 minutes until golden brown. They should hold their shape, but if they do not, hold a little longer with the tongs. Drain on absorbent kitchen paper.

Put a layer of lettuce in each taco shell. Spoon Picadillo onto lettuce, then top with onion, tomato and another layer of lettuce to finish. Serve immediately.

Serves 6.

ENSALADA MEXICANA

250 g (8 oz) small new potatoes
2 large carrots, diced
1 turnip, diced
½ small cauliflower, divided into florets
3 small gherkins
1 tablespoon capers
6 black olives, stoned
60 ml (2 fl oz / ¼ cup) mayonnaise
1 teaspoon Dijon mustard

Dressing:
90 ml (3 fl oz / ⅓ cup) olive oil
2 tablespoons wine vinegar
salt and pepper

Boil potatoes in lightly salted water for about 10 minutes until just tender. Drain and set aside. Boil carrots and turnip in lightly salted water for 8-10 minutes until just tender. Drain and set aside. Cook the cauliflower in lightly salted boiling water for 5 minutes. Drain. While still warm, mix together all the vegetables in a bowl.

Put oil, vinegar, salt and pepper in a screw-top jar and shake well. Pour over the vegetables and toss gently. Put gherkins in the centre of a serving plate. Place capers and olives around the gherkins. Arrange vegetables around the outside of the plate. Put mayonnaise and mustard into a small bowl and mix well. Pour a trail of the mayonnaise mixture over vegetables. Serve at room temperature.

Serves 4-6.

— CHILLED VEGETABLE SALAD —

500 g (1 lb) courgettes (zucchini), cut into 1 cm
　(½ in) slices
250 g (8 oz) cooked, or thawed frozen peas
1 stalk celery, sliced
1 tablespoon chilli powder
1 small clove garlic
¼ teaspoon cumin
1 teaspoon fresh thyme or ½ teaspoon dried thyme
60 ml (2 fl oz / ¼ cup) water
60 ml (2 fl oz / ¼ cup) red wine vinegar
1 bay leaf
salt and pepper
60 ml (2 fl oz / ¼ cup) olive oil

In a large bowl, mix courgettes (zucchini), peas
and celery. Put the chilli, garlic, cumin and
thyme in a small bowl and mash to a paste.
Carefully stir into the large bowl. Put water
and vinegar in a small saucepan and bring to
the boil. Pour over the vegetables and stir in
bay leaf, salt and pepper. Cover bowl and leave
at room temperature for 48 hours. Two hours
before serving, chill salad.

Stir in the oil, remove bay leaf, adjust seasoning and serve as an accompaniment to meat
and bean dishes.

Serves 4.

—— POTATO & HERB SALAD ——

500 g (1 lb) potatoes, sliced
1 tablespoon finely chopped fresh coriander
1 tablespoon olive oil
30 ml (1 fl oz / 2 tablespoons) malt vinegar
salt and pepper
2 spring onions, roughly chopped
8 black olives, halved and stoned

Steam potatoes over boiling salted water for
7-10 minutes until tender. Put into a serving
bowl.

In a screwtop jar, shake together coriander,
oil, vinegar, salt and pepper. Sprinkle with
spring onions and arrange the olives to garnish.

Serves 4-6.

AVOCADO & CAULIFLOWER SALAD

1 small cauliflower, divided into florets
30 ml (1 fl oz / 2 tablespoons) white wine vinegar
salt and pepper
4 small ripe avocado pears
60 g (2 oz / 1 ½ cups) ground almonds
½ teaspoon ground nutmeg
6 radishes, thinly sliced, to garnish

Cook the cauliflower in boiling salted water for 5 minutes. Drain and cool then put in a large bowl. Sprinkle with vinegar and salt and pepper and set aside.

Cut the avocados in half, remove the stones and scoop the flesh into a bowl; mash. Stir in the almonds, nutmeg, salt and pepper. Mix well. Carefully combine with cauliflower, cover and chill. Serve garnished with radishes.

Serves 4.

—— FRIED SWEETCORN ——

30 ml (1 fl oz / 2 tablespoons) oil
1 small onion, finely chopped
½ small green pepper (capsicum), seeded and cut into thin strips
½ small red pepper (capsicum), seeded and cut into thin strips
2 tablespoons chopped fresh coriander
1 green chilli, seeded and finely chopped
350 g (12 oz) sweetcorn kernels
125 g (4 oz) button mushrooms, wiped
salt and pepper
8 sprigs coriander

Heat the oil in a heavy frying pan. Add onion, peppers (capsicums) and chilli. Cook gently for 5 minutes, stirring occasionally, until soft. Stir in sweetcorn, mushrooms and ground pepper. Cook gently for 5 minutes, stirring occasionally.

Transfer to a warmed serving dish and garnish with coriander.

Serves 6.

CHILLIES RELLENOS

6 medium green peppers (capsicums)
30 g (1 oz/2 tablespoons) butter
1 medium onion, finely chopped
2 cloves garlic, finely chopped
500 g (1 lb) lean minced pork
60 g (2 oz/¹/₂ cup) walnuts, finely chopped
1 medium cooking apple
2 peaches
90 g (3 oz/¹/₂ cup) seedless raisins
3 tablespoons finely chopped fresh coriander
1 teaspoon ground cinnamon
¹/₂ teaspoon ground cloves
salt and pepper
30 g (1 oz/2 tablespoons) sugar
60 ml (2 fl oz/¹/₄ cup) dry sherry
315 ml (10 fl oz/1 ¹/₄ cups) hot water
Wheat or Corn Tortillas and Mexican rice to serve

Sauce:
175 g (6 oz) soft full-fat cheese
155 ml (5 fl oz/²/₃ cup) thick sour cream
60 g (2 oz/¹/₂ cup) walnuts, finely chopped
1 clove garlic, crushed
¹/₄ teaspoon ground cumin.

Pre-heat grill to the hottest setting. Put the peppers (capsicums) on a baking tray and place them about 7.5 cm (3 in) below the grill for about 7 minutes, turning so they char evenly. When cool enough to handle, peel off all the skin. Discard stems, white membrane, and seeds; set aside.

Melt the butter in a frying pan and gently fry the onion and garlic for about 7 minutes until soft. Add the pork, and cook 5 minutes, stirring constantly. Peel, core and chop the apple; stone and chop the peaches. Stir apple, peaches, raisins, walnuts, 1 tablespoon coriander, cinnamon, cloves, salt, pepper, sugar, sherry and hot water, into pan. Simmer for 10 minutes or until the liquid has evaporated. Remove from the heat, cover and keep hot.

To make the sauce, in a bowl, stir together soft cheese, sour cream, walnuts, garlic and cumin. Season with salt.

Fill the peppers (capsicums) with pork mixture, spoon the sauce over the top, and garnish with remaining coriander. Serve immediately with Tortillas or Mexican Rice.

Serves 6.

CARROTS WITH TEQUILA

500 g (1 lb) carrots
60 g (2 oz / 4 tablespoons) butter
¼ teaspoon dried dill weed, crushed
salt and pepper
60 ml (2 fl oz / ¼ cup) tequila

Cut carrots diagonally into 5 mm (¼ in) thick slices. Melt butter in a frying pan over a low heat. Add the carrots. Increase the heat to medium and cook the carrots for 10 minutes, stirring occasionally. Add the dill weed, salt and pepper. Mix well. Increase the heat.

Pour the tequila over the carrots, then ignite using a lighted taper. When the flames have died down, stir, and serve immediately.

Serves 4.

ENCHILADAS WITH PEPPERS

60 ml (2 fl oz / ¼ cup) sunflower oil
1 large onion, chopped
1 clove garlic
1 fresh green chilli, finely chopped
2 red peppers (capsicums), seeded and chopped
4 large tomatoes, blanched, skinned and chopped
1 bay leaf
2 tablespoons chopped fresh coriander
250 ml (8 fl oz / 1 cup) beef stock
125 ml (4 fl oz / ½ cup) thick sour cream
salt
½ quantity Cooked Tomato Sauce
12 Wheat Tortillas
60 g (2 oz) Cheddar cheese, grated

Heat half the oil in a heavy frying pan. Fry the onion, garlic and chilli gently for 5-7 minutes until soft. Add the peppers (capsicums) and continue to cook until just tender. Add the tomatoes, bay leaf, coriander and stock; cook 1-2 minutes. Remove from the heat and stir in the sour cream and salt. Divide tomato mixture between the tortillas; placing it in the centre of each.

Fold over edges, sides to middle; then fold the ends under to enclose completely. Secure with wooden cocktail sticks. In a saucepan, gently heat the Tomato Sauce, stirring occasionally and keep warm. Meanwhile, heat a heavy frying pan with remaining oil and fry the sealed side down, for 2 minutes each side until golden. Turn and fry the other side. Transfer to a warmed serving dish. Spoon the Tomato Sauce over and sprinkle with cheese.

Serves 6.

MEXICAN RICE

375 g (12 oz) long-grain rice
2 tablespoons sunflower oil
1 large onion, chopped
2 cloves garlic, finely chopped
4-6 fresh hot red or green chillies
315 g (10 oz) tomatoes, blanched, peeled, seeded
  and chopped
1 litre (32 fl oz / 4 cups) chicken stock
salt and pepper
60 g (2 oz) cooked or thawed frozen peas
fresh coriander sprigs to garnish

Put the rice into a bowl, cover with boiling water and leave for 30 minutes. Drain. Leave in a sieve for about 1 hour until dry. Heat the oil in a heavy frying pan. Over a low heat, stir in the rice until all the grains are well coated with oil. Add onion, garlic and chillies. Cook for about 4 minutes until the onion is transparent and the rice is golden. Add the tomatoes and stock, season with salt and pepper, cover and simmer for 20-30 minutes or until the liquid has been absorbed and the rice is tender and fluffy; add peas 5 minutes before end of cooking.

If softer rice is preferred, stir in a little more stock after 20 minutes and continue cooking until additional liquid has been absorbed. Transfer to a warmed serving dish and garnish with coriander.

Serves 6-8.

KIDNEY BEAN STEW

1 onion, halved
1 tablespoon oil
1 tablespoon finely chopped coriander
1 chilli, skinned and finely chopped
1 small tomato, seeded and finely chopped
½ quantity Basic Beans
salt
60 g (2 oz) Cheddar cheese, grated, to garnish

Finely chop half the onion. Heat oil in a saucepan. Add chopped onion and fry gently until soft but not brown. Add coriander, chilli and tomato. Cook for 5 minutes. Stir in the beans and season with salt. Heat through. Remove from the heat and leave, covered, for several hours to allow the flavours to develop. To serve, re-heat, stirring constantly. Slice remaining onion half.

Transfer beans to individual warmed serving dishes. Garnish with onion slices and cheese.

Serves 4.

GREEN RICE

1 large green pepper (capsicum), seeded and
  chopped
1 small onion, roughly chopped
2 cloves garlic
4 tablespoons fresh chopped coriander
45 ml (1 ½ fl oz / 3 tablespoons) oil
250 g (8 oz) long-grain rice
625 ml (20 fl oz / 2 ½ cups) chicken stock
salt and pepper

Put the pepper (capsicum), onion, garlic and
coriander in a blender or food processor
and process until finely chopped. Heat 1
tablespoon oil in a small saucepan. Stir in
the onion mixture and cook, stirring, for 3
minutes. Heat remaining oil in a heavy frying
pan. Add rice. Stir over a medium heat for
about 3-4 minutes until light brown.

Add the onion mixture, stock, salt and pepper. Bring to the boil, cover, then simmer for
10 minutes until liquid is absorbed. Reduce
heat to very low and steam, still covered, for
30-40 minutes until rice is tender. Add more
stock if necessary to keep rice moist. Adjust
seasoning. Transfer to a warmed serving dish.

Serves 4-6.

SPINACH WITH PIMENTO

1 kg (2 lb) fresh spinach
60 ml (2 fl oz / ¼ cup) oil
1 clove garlic, crushed
30 g (1 oz / 2 tablespoons) butter
30 g (1 oz / 2 tablespoons) plain (all purpose) flour
155 ml (5 fl oz / ⅔ cup) milk
salt and pepper
2 hard-boiled eggs, sliced
2 large red peppers (capsicums), seeded and cut into
  strips

Rinse spinach thoroughly and shake off excess
water. Heat oil in a large saucepan. Add garlic
and stir for 1 minute. Add spinach and cook
over medium heat, stirring constantly, until
soft. Drain and chop.

Heat butter in the pan, stir in the flour and
cook for 2 minutes, stirring. Gradually stir the
milk until the mixture is very thick. Cook for
2 minutes still stirring. Add spinach and heat
through. Season to taste. Transfer to warm
serving dish. Garnish with eggs and peppers.

Serves 4.

ORANGE BREAD PUDDING

10 slices day-old bread, crusts removed, cubed
375 g (12 oz) can mandarin oranges, drained
60 g (2 oz / 1/3 cup) seedless raisins
60 g (2 oz / 1/2 cup) chopped almonds
60 g (2 oz / 1/4 cup) butter, diced
625 ml (20 fl oz / 2 1/2 cups) milk
3 eggs
125 g (4 oz / 2/3 cup) dark soft brown sugar
1/2 teaspoon freshly grated nutmeg
1/2 teaspoon ground cinnamon
few drops of vanilla essence

Pre-heat oven 180°C (350°F/Gas 4). Grease a 23 x 33 cm (9 x 13 in) shallow baking dish. Mix together the bread, oranges, raisins and nuts. Transfer to the baking tin.

In a saucepan, gently heat the butter and the milk until the butter has melted, then bring to just below simmering point, but do not boil. Remove from the heat.

In a large bowl, stir together the eggs, sugar, spices and essence. Stir in the milk and butter then slowly pour into the bread mixture so that it soaks and flows through.

Bake for 45 minutes, until set in centre and golden brown and crisp on top.

Serves 6.

CARAMEL CUSTARD

250 g (8 oz / 1 cup) caster sugar
2 tablespoons water
940 ml (30 fl oz / 3 3/4 cups) milk
few drops of vanilla essence
3 eggs
6 egg yolks

Pre-heat oven 150°C (300°F/Gas 2). Put half the sugar and the water into a heavy-based saucepan, place over a low heat and stir gently until the sugar has dissolved. Increase the heat and boil rapidly without stirring until syrup turns golden.

Pour into 8-9 individual ramekin dishes or dariole moulds, tipping them to coat the base and 1 cm (1/2 in) up the sides. Heat the milk in a heavy-based saucepan over a low heat. Add remaining sugar, salt and vanilla essence. Heat, stirring frequently, until sugar has dissolved, about 2-3 minutes. Beat the eggs and egg yolks together in a bowl, then stir in the milk. Strain through a sieve onto the caramel in the ramekin dishes or moulds. Place in a roasting tin and pour boiling water around the dishes. Cover them with buttered greaseproof paper.

Bake for 45 minutes until lightly set in the centre. Remove the dishes from the tin, cool, then chill. To serve, dip bottom of dishes or moulds in hot water, then stand for a few minutes. Shake gently to loosen and turn onto individual serving plates.

Serves 8-9

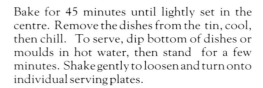

CINNAMON ORANGES

3 oranges, peeled and thinly sliced crossways
60 g (2 oz / ¼ cup) caster sugar
¼ teaspoon ground cinnamon

Place oranges in a serving bowl. Mix sugar and cinnamon together in a small bowl; sprinkle over the oranges.

Cover the bowl and refrigerate for at least 1 hour.

Serves 4.

LEMON TEQUILA SOUFFLE

3 lemons
3 eggs, separated
90 g (3 oz / ¹/3 cup) caster sugar
4 teaspoons powdered gelatine
3 tablespoons tequila
155 ml (5 fl oz / ²/3 cup) double (thick) cream

Decoration:
155 ml (5 fl oz / ²/3 cup) double (thick) cream
fresh mint leaves

Tie around a 15 cm (6 in) soufflé dish a band of greaseproof paper that extends 5 cm (2 in) above edge of the dish. Grate rind from all lemons; squeeze juice from 2. Brush dish and paper with oil.
In a bowl, placed over a saucepan of hot water, whisk the egg yolks, sugar and lemon rind until thick. Put the tequila into a small bowl, sprinkle the gelatine over the top and leave for 5 minutes to soften. Place the bowl over a saucepan of hot water and stir until the gelatine has dissolved. Remove bowl from the pan; allow gelatine to cool slightly, stir in lemon juice, then stir slowly into the lemon mixture.

Whisk the cream until soft peaks form, then gently fold into the lemon mixture until just evenly mixed. Set aside until nearly set. Whisk the egg whites until stiff then fold carefully into the lemon mixture. Spoon into the prepared dish. Chill until set. To decorate, whip cream, spoon into piping bag fitted with star nozzle. Pipe onto soufflé and arrange mint leaves.

Serves 6.

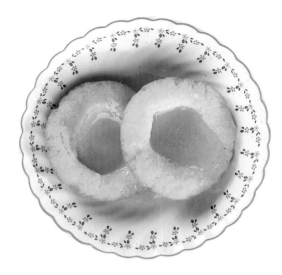

HONEYED FRITTERS

250 g (8 oz / 2 cups) plain (all purpose) flour
½ teaspoon baking powder
salt
30 g (1 oz / 2 tablespoons) caster sugar
1 egg, beaten
30 g (1 oz / 2 tablespoons) butter, melted
125 ml (4 fl oz / ½ cup) milk
sunflower oil for deep frying

Syrup:
2 tablespoons clear honey
1 tablespoon rum
½ teaspoon ground cinnamon
1 tablespoon butter

Sift flour, baking powder and salt into a large bowl. Stir in sugar, add the egg, butter and enough milk to form a soft, not sticky dough. Turn onto a lightly floured surface and knead until smooth. Divide dough into 8-12 pieces; shape each into a ball. Cover and leave for 30 minutes. On a lightly floured surface, shape the balls into flat cakes; using the back of a metal spoon, make a shallow indentation in the top of each cake. Heat a deep fat frying pan two-thirds full of oil to 190°C (375°F). Fry a few at a time for 5 minutes until golden brown and puffy. Drain on absorbent kitchen paper.

To make the syrup, place all the ingredients in a heavy-based saucepan. Bring slowly to the boil, stirring frequently. Simmer, stirring occasionally, for 20 minutes, or until the mixture thickens to a syrup. Remove the cinnamon stick. Serve the fritters in individual bowls with syrup poured over.

Serves 6.

MANGOES WITH CREAM

250 ml (8 fl oz / 1 cup) water
125 g (4 oz / ½ cup) sugar
1 cm (½ in) cinnamon stick
3 mangoes, peeled and thickly sliced lengthways
few drops of vanilla essence
155 ml (5 fl oz / ⅔ cup) double (thick) cream
60 ml (2 fl oz / ¼ cup) rum

Put water, half the sugar, and the cinnamon stick into a heavy-based saucepan. Bring to the boil, then simmer for 20-30 minutes, stirring occasionally, until the syrup thickens. Add the mango slices to the syrup and simmer for 5-10 minutes until just tender. Remove the cinnamon stick and add the vanilla essence. Transfer to a serving dish and allow to cool.

Cover and chill. Whip together the cream and remaining sugar until soft peaks form. Fold in the rum. Serve in a separate bowl to accompany the mangoes.

Serves 6.

CHERRY CHIMICHANGAS

2 tablespoons arrowroot
315 ml (10 fl oz / 1 1/4 cups) water
2 tablespoons granulated sugar
8 oz (250 g) ripe red cherries, rinsed, stalks removed, stoned
grated rind of 1 orange
8 Wheat Tortillas
90 g (3 oz / 1/3 cup) butter
60 g (2 oz) icing sugar
60 g (2 oz) toasted slivered almonds to decorate

In a saucepan mix the arrowroot with a little of the water to a smooth paste. Gradually stir in the remaining water, then the granulated sugar. Bring to the boil over a medium heat, stirring. Simmer for 2 minutes. Remove from the heat and stir in the cherries and orange rind. Divide cherry mixture between the tortillas. Fold each tortilla in half, then in half again.

Heat the butter in a frying pan. Add two filled tortillas and fry gently for 2 1/2 minutes each side until golden brown.

Transfer to a warmed serving plate and keep warm. Repeat with remaining tortillas, adding more butter if necessary. Sieve over icing sugar and decorate with toasted almonds.

Serves 4-8.

PUMPKIN IN SYRUP

1 kg (2 lb) pumpkin weighed with skin and seeds
1 lemon
315 ml (10 fl oz / 1 1/4 cups) water
60 g (2 oz / 1/4 cup) granulated sugar
1 orange
1 tablespoon Cointreau

Peel the pumpkin and discard the seeds. Cut the flesh into bite-size pieces. Squeeze the juice from the lemon; reserve the peel. Put the water, sugar and lemon juice into a saucepan. Bring to the boil, stirring constantly.

Peel the orange and reserve the flesh. Wash the orange and lemon peel under hot water to rub away all white pith. Add peel to syrup. Add pumpkin. Simmer for 10 minutes or until the pumpkin is tender. Divide the orange into segments then chop into small pieces. Put into a serving bowl. Using a slotted spoon, lift the pumpkin from the syrup, and mix with the orange in the bowl. Lift the peels from the syrup, and cut into fine shreds; reserve for decoration.

Boil the remaining syrup until reduced to 2 tablespoons. Remove from the heat and stir in the Cointreau. Pour over the fruit. Leave until cold, then cover and chill well. Decorate with shredded peel.

Serves 6.

CARAMEL RUM APPLES

185 g (6 oz / 3/4 cup) butter, chopped
125 g (4 oz / 1/2 cup) light soft brown sugar
2 teaspoons lemon juice
3 tablespoons water
6 medium eating apples
2 tablespoons rum
1/2 teaspoon ground cinnamon
ice cream or cream to serve

CHOCOLATE ORANGE MOUSSE

375 g (12 oz) plain (dark) chocolate, broken
4 tablespoons water
1 tablespoon butter
1 tablespoon orange liqueur
4 eggs, separated
155 ml (5 fl oz / 2/3 cup) double (thick) cream,
  whipped to decorate

Put the butter into a large saucepan then place over a low heat until melted. Stir in sugar, lemon juice and water and simmer gently, stirring ocasionally until the sugar has dissolved; then simmer without stirring until slightly thickened and golden, about 10-12 minutes.

Put the chocolate in a bowl with the water. Place the bowl over a pan of gently simmering water and leave the chocolate to melt, stirring occasionally. Remove the pan from the heat and stir the chocolate for 5 minutes. Remove the bowl from the pan and stir the butter and liquer into the chocolate.

Peel the apples; using an apple corer, remove the cores, then slice the apples into rings. Add the rum, cinnamon and apples, making sure the apples are thoroughly coated with the syrup. Simmer until the apples are soft, about 5 minutes. Transfer to a serving dish. Serve warm with ice cream or cream

Serves 4-6.

In a clean bowl, whisk the egg whites until stiff. Beat the yolks into the slightly cooled chocolate mixture, then gently fold in whites until just evenly mixed. Spoon the mousse into individual glasses and refrigerate until set, about 1 hour. Pipe whipped cream over to decorate.

Serves 6.

ALMOND JELLY

4 tablespoons water
1 1/2 tablespoons powdered gelatine
250 ml (8 fl oz / 1 cup) boiling water
250 g (8 oz / 1 cup) granulated sugar
few drops of almond essence
6 egg whites
salt
155 g (5 oz/1 cup) blanched halved almonds

Custard:
1 litre (32 fl oz/4 cups) milk
6 egg yolks
60 g (2 oz/1/4 cup) caster sugar
few drops vanilla essence
100 ml (3 1/2 fl oz/1/3 cup) double (thick) cream

Rinse the inside of a 1.5 L (2½ pint) mould with cold water. Leave upside down to drain well. Put water into a small bowl, sprinkle over gelatine and leave for 5 minutes to soften. Stir in boiling water, until the gelatine has dissolved. Stir in sugar to dissolve; add almond essence. Refrigerate until beginning to thicken, about 10 minutes; whisk until frothy.

In a large bowl, whisk egg whites until stiff. Gently fold into gelatine mixture. Pour half into prepared mould. Reserve some almonds for decoration; sprinkle the remainder over the mixture. Spoon remaining mixture over. Refrigerate at least 4 hours, preferably overnight.

45 minutes before serving, make the custard. Heat milk slowly to just below simmering point. Meanwhile, in a bowl placed over a saucepan of hot water, whisk egg yolks with sugar until thick. Strain milk onto yolks, stirring so mixture remains smooth.

Cook, stirring constantly with a wooden spoon, until lightly thickened. Stir in essence, remove from heat, and cool for 10 minutes.

Whip cream until stiff. Fold into custard; chill for 30 minutes. Unmould the jelly, sprinkle with the reserved almonds and pour the custard around.

Serves 8.

COMPOTE

185 g (6 oz / 1 ¹/₃ cups) dried no-soak apricots
125 g (4 oz / ²/₃ cup) stoned no-soak prunes
125 g (4 oz / ²/₃ cup) dried peaches or pears,
    chopped
125 g (4 oz / ²/₃ cup) seedless raisins
60 g (2 oz / ¹/₂ cup) blanched split almonds
5 cm (2 in) cinnamon stick
4 whole cloves
60 g (2 oz / ¹/₃ cup) toasted walnut halves, see
    Note

Put dried fruits, almonds, cinnamon and cloves into a saucepan, cover with water. Cover pan and simmer for 15 minutes or until fruits are tender but not mushy. Remove from heat and cool to lukewarm. Remove cinnamon and cloves.

Spoon into individual glasses or a serving bowl. Cover and chill. Sprinkle with chopped walnuts.

Serves 6.

Note: To toast walnuts, spread on a baking sheet and place in an oven preheated to 160°C (325°F/Gas 3) for 15 minutes, turning frequently; watch closely to prevent burning.

PECAN & ALMOND CAKES

2 eggs, separated
125 g (4 oz/ ¹/₂ cup) caster sugar
few drops of vanilla essence
90 g (3 oz / ³/₄ cup) plain (all-purpose) flour
1 teaspoon baking powder
30 g (1 oz / ¹/₄ cup) mixed pecan nuts and
    almonds, chopped
2 tablespoons icing sugar
Mexican Hot Chocolate to serve

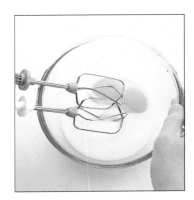

Pre-heat oven to 150°C (300°F/Gas 2). Grease 12 individual bun tins. Whisk egg yolks with sugar until thick and pale. Gently stir in essence. Sift together flour and baking powder over the surface of the egg yolk mixture, then fold in.

In a clean bowl, whisk egg whites until stiff; fold gently into the egg yolk mixture. Carefully fold in the nuts. Divide between the prepared bun tins and bake for 15 minutes. Sieve icing sugar over and serve warm with Mexican Hot Chocolate.

Makes 12.

CINNAMON COOKIES

250 g (8 oz) soft margarine
125 g (4 oz / ½ cup) caster sugar
1 teaspoon vanilla essence
350 g (12 oz / 3 cups) plain (all-purpose) flour
2 teaspoons ground cinnamon
salt
250 g (8 oz / 1 ½ cups) icing sugar

Pre-heat oven to 180°C (350°F/Gas 4).

Grease 2 baking sheets. Beat together margarine, sugar and vanilla essence. Stir in flour and 1 teaspoon cinnamon to make a soft dough. Cover and refrigerate for 1 hour.

Form mixture into 2.5 cm (1 in) balls and place on a prepared baking sheet, leaving space between each one. Bake for 15 minutes. Remove from the oven, leave on the baking sheets for a few minutes, then transfer to a wire rack to cool. Mix together the icing sugar and remaining cinnamon; sieve over the cookies.

Makes 24 cookies.

APRICOT & COCONUT BALLS

185 g (6 oz / 1 ⅓ cups) dried apricots, finely chopped
125 g (4 oz / 2 ½ cups) flaked coconut
60 g (2 oz / ½ cup) blanched almonds, finely chopped
few drops vanilla essence
half of 397 g (14 oz) can condensed milk
icing sugar to coat

Put apricots, coconut, almonds and vanilla essence into a bowl; mix together. Stir in enough condensed milk to bind to a stiff mixture.

Shape into balls about the size of a large hazelnut, roll in sieved icing sugar, and place in small paper cases.

Makes 24 sweets.

PECAN CANDY

250 g (8 oz / 1 1/2 cups) soft dark brown sugar
155 ml (5 fl oz / 2/3 cup) milk
3 tablespoons light maple syrup
salt
125 g (4 oz / 1 1/4 cups) pecan halves
40 g (1 oz / 2 tablespoons) butter, softened
few drops vanilla essence

Line a baking tray with waxed paper. Put sugar, milk, maple syrup and salt into a large heavy based saucepan. Stir with a wooden spoon over a medium heat, until sugar has dissolved then bring to the boil. Add nuts. Cook until the soft ball stage, 115°C (238°F). Remove from heat. Cool until lukewarm. Stir in butter and essence and continue to stir for 2 minutes until mixture begins to thicken and become creamy.

Drop teaspoonsfuls of the mixture onto the waxed paper. Leave to set. Store in a plastic bag in refrigerator for 2-3 days.

Makes 18 sweets.

Note: To test for soft ball stage without a sugar thermometer, remove pan from heat, dip bottom in cold water. Drop a small amount of syrup into very cold water, roll it into a ball, and remove. The ball should flatten under slight pressure.

— MEXICAN HOT CHOCOLATE —

250 g (8 oz) plain (dark) chocolate, broken
940 ml (30 fl oz / 3 3/4 cups) milk
1/4 teaspoon ground cinnamon
few drops of vanilla essence

Put the chocolate in a large bowl and place over a saucepan of hot water until melted. Whisk in the hot milk, then pour into a saucepan. Add cinnamon and vanilla. Bring to the boil. Lower the heat and whisk for 2 minutes.

Remove from the heat and whisk until bubbles form on top of the liquid. Serve hot in individual cups, dividing the foam equally, or leave until cold; whisk again before serving.

Serves 4.

CAFE DE OLLA

1.25 litres (40 fl oz / 9 cups) water
2.5 cm (1 in) piece cinnamon stick
2 cloves
60 g (2 oz / ¼ cup) muscovado sugar
4 tablespoons freshly ground coffee

Put the water, cinnamon and cloves into a saucepan and bring to the boil. Lower the heat, add the sugar and stir until dissolved. Stir in the coffee and simmer for 2 minutes.

Turn off the heat and allow to stand, covered, for about 5 minutes until all the coffee has settled. Strain into individual mugs.

Serves 4.

MARGARITA

1 lime, halved
salt
crushed ice
60 ml (2 fl oz / ¼ cup) tequila
1 tablespoon Triple Sec or Cointreau
wedge of lime to serve

Rub the rim of a chilled cocktail glass with one of the lime halves then dip into salt. Add crushed ice to a cocktail shaker or mixing glass. Squeeze the juice from the remaining lime half.

Pour into the shaker or glass with the tequila and Triple Sec or Cointreau. Shake or stir well. Strain into the glass. Serve with a wedge of lime to squeeze into drink.

Serves 1.

TEQUILA SUNRISE

60 ml (2 fl oz / ¼ cup) tequila
150 ml (5 fl oz / ⅔ cup) fresh orange juice
1 tablespoon grenadine
1 teaspoon fresh lime juice
crushed ice
cocktail cherry to decorate

Pour tequila, orange juice, grenadine and lime juice into a blender or food processor; mix well. Put crushed ice into a tall, chilled glass.

Strain tequila mixture over the ice. Decorate with a cocktail cherry on cocktail stick.

Serves 1.

LIMONADA

1 lemon, quartered
1 litre (32 fl oz / 4 cups) cold water
185 g (6 oz / ⅔ cup) granulated sugar
sprigs of mint to decorate

Put the lemon, sugar and 315 ml (10 fl oz / 1 ½ cups) water in a blender or food processor and process for 40 seconds. Strain into a serving jug.

Pour the remaining water through the strainer into the jug. Chill well. Serve over ice-cubes and decorate with mint.

Serves 6.

INDEX

Almond Jelly, 58
Almond Sauce, 42
Apricot & Coconut Balls, 60
Avocado & Cauliflower Salad, 48
Acovado Soup, 15

Baked Spiced Fish, 28
Basic Beans, 11
Bean Dip, 18

Café de Olla, 62
Caramel Custard, 53
Caramel Rum Apples, 57
Carnitas, 34
Carrots with Tequila, 50
Ceviche, 18
Chayote Salad, 44
Cheese-Filled Enchiladas, 25
Cherry Chimichangas, 56
Chicken Empanadas, 35
Chicken Enchiladas, 36
Chicken Tortilla Soup, 14
Chilled Vegetable Salad, 47
Chilli Con Carne, 38
Chilli Fish, 31
Chillies Rellenos, 49
Chimichangas, 24
Chocolate Orange Mousse, 57
Chorizo & Cheese Pancakes, 40
Christmas Salad, 44
Cinnamon Cookies, 60
Cinnamon Oranges, 54
Cod Yucatan-Style, 31
Compote, 59
Cooked Tomato Sauce, 12
Corn Soufflé, 22
Corn Soup, 16
Corn Tortillas, 10
Crab Enchiladas, 27

Egg-Filled Enchiladas, 24
Eggs Vallejo-Style, 22
Eggs with Potatoes & Ham, 23
Empanadas, 35

Enchiladas with Peppers, 50
Ensalada Mexicana, 46

Fish in Garlic Sauce, 30
Fish in Green Sauce, 28
Fried Sweetcorn, 48

Green Chilli Relish, 42
Green Rice, 52
Grilled Steak, 39
Guacamole, 17

Honeyed Fritters, 55
Hot Chilli Sauce, 41
Hot Fish Burritos, 29

Kidney Bean Stew, 51

Lamb with Red Wine, 39
Lemon Tequila Soufflé, 54
Limonada, 63

Mangoes with Cream, 55
Margarita, 62
Marinated Mushrooms, 17
Meatball Kebabs, 19
Meatballs in Hot Sauce, 37
Mexicali Chicken, 32
Mexican Hot Chocolate, 61
Mexican Pork Chops, 34
Mexican Rice, 51
Mole Poblano, 33

Nachos, 20

Orange Bread Pudding, 53

Pecan & Almond Cakes, 59
Pecan Candy, 61
Picadillo, 13
Pork Coastal-Style, 36
Potato & Herb Salad, 47
Prawns with Chilli Cheese, 16
Pumpkin in Syrup, 56

Quesadillas, 25

Ranch-Style Eggs, 23
Red Snapper in Coriander, 32
Red Snapper Veracruz-Style, 30
Refried Beans, 12
Rum-Barbecued Steak, 38

Salad Dressing, 43
Salsa Fresca, 41
Salsa Verde, 43
Savoury Tamales, 21
Sopa Frijoles, 15
Spinach with Pimento, 52
Spring Onion Salad, 45
Stuffed Eggs, 19
Stuffed Roast Beef Rolls, 20

Taco Shell Salad, 46
Tequila Sunrise, 63
Tomato Salad, 45
Tortillas with Cream & Cheese, 26
Tuna Casserole, 26

Vegetable Soup, 14
Vermicelli Soup, 13

Wheat Tortillas, 11